Antiquarian Pursuits

Antiquarian Pursuits

SOUTHERN ART FROM THE HOLDINGS OF ROBERT M. HICKLIN JR., INC.

in celebration of the gallery's twentieth anniversary

WITH AN ESSAY BY ESTILL CURTIS PENNINGTON

Robert M. Hicklin Jr., Inc. • 509 East St. John St. • Spartanburg, South Carolina 29302 • (803)583-9847 • FAX (803)583-8338

Design
ANNE MORGAN JONES

Lithography
BLUE RIDGE PRINTING

Photography
BLAKE PRAYTOR

Editor
LYNNE BLACKMAN

Assistant Editor
HOLLY WATTERS

Antiquarian Pursuits
COPYRIGHT © 1992
ROBERT M. HICKLIN JR., INC.
SPARTANBURG, SOUTH CAROLINA
Library of Congress
catalog card number:
92-071543

ISBN 0-9632836-0-X

Cover
THE CULPEPPER HUNT
John J. Porter
PAGE 42

A VIEW OF THE GALLERY
PAGE vi

Table of Contents

Some Thoughts of a Southern Picture Dealer After Twenty Years	vii
Robert M. Hicklin, Jr.	
Acknowledgements	viii
Antiquarian Pursuits: Episodes in Southern Art History	1
Estill Curtis Pennington	
Select Bibliography	22
Acknowledgements	24
Southern Painting and Sculpture from the Gallery's Collection	25
Index of Artists	88

The library and archives of Robert M. Hicklin Jr., Inc. are open without fee to scholars and collectors with an interest in the study and advancement of Southern art history.

SOME THOUGHTS OF
a Southern Picture Dealer
AFTER TWENTY YEARS

To awaken and heighten an interest in the realm of creative endeavor that I have chosen as my life's work requires a savoring of that distinctive blend of ingredients found in the simmering gumbo pot of Southern art. There have been many contributions to the color, flavor, and texture of the broth by art historians, collectors, and dealers–individuals whose passion and expertise have enlarged and enhanced not only the art, but our understanding of it as well. Their study and support serves as the roux which makes our appreciation whole and unique.

To my eye, the recurring themes which proliferate in the larger arena of American art are evident in every aspect of the Southern paintings and sculpture we see. But Southern art has been and continues to be created by those who are of the South. Whether native or foreign they are nurtured by this region's strongly indigenous culture. What we have collectively determined to be the art of the American South ranges from the sentimentality of William Aiken Walker's figure studies of humble black sharecroppers to the grandeur of Ferdinand Richardt's magnificent view of Harper's Ferry. Though varied in style and subject matter, each suggests a link between the Southern setting and the ways of the Southern people. One depicts a South depleted, while the other evokes a land of promise and natural splendor.

It has been my privilege to help season and stir this pot for some twenty years. I know now that a taste for the contents depends as much upon a knowledge of the art as it does upon the people, the landscape, and its products. I have gained much from the talents of the artists whose works are depicted and described herein. This has been imparted to me by the antiquarians and connoisseurs who have gone before. A sampling of these mentors is documented in Mr. Pennington's essay which follows. But it is the living, breathing Jay Altmayers of this land, along with Estill Curtis Pennington, Cynthia Seibels, and so many others who contribute to the knowledge of and enthusiasm for Southern art that make me know that my pursuit is worthy.

Robert M. Hicklin, Jr.

Acknowledgements

This organization continues to benefit from deep-rooted associations with many people who have proven their dedication to it and to Southern art. Kim Tuck and Holly Watters have collectively guided us through half of our twenty year history. Jane Hicklin has worked diligently and done with less than anyone who might have worked for wages. These are the full-timers, certainly those hardest to thank.

Others have worked with us before and it is with pleasure that we acknowledge them again. Anne Jones designed this catalog, as well as most of our other publications. Her creative style and distinctive touch suit us very well. Blake Praytor, our photographer, skillfully shot each of the works illustrated and continues to photograph all of the paintings that pass through our hands. Cynthia Seibels meticulously researches most works the gallery handles and produces essays on those items and the context of their Southerness and that of their creators. These essays are the basis of our reference files and their sheer volume is quickly distinguishing them as a resource of greatest substance for students of Southern art history. Mr. Pennington had access to these in the creation of his entries in *Antiquarian Pursuits*. Lynne Blackman has edited this work and beautifully coordinated the efforts of each of the above.

Almost two years ago I told Mr. Pennington that I would soon celebrate my twentieth year in art which relates to the American South. My query for thoughts on a suitable response to this event was, after an appropriate period of consideration, the outline of an essay as it appears herein. That essay and all but two of the catalog entries are from his pen. There is no greater mind working in the field of Southern art history.

This publication is a tribute to each of those named above and, more importantly, to those who have found our endeavors worth supporting for these twenty years. They are hardly without number and surely they know who they are. Hundreds of individuals, no less than sixty public institutions, and a few companies with real Southern roots have helped us sustain and grow. We are proud of our associations with each of you and trust that you will find merit in *Antiquarian Pursuits*.

Robert M. Hicklin, Jr.

Antiquarian Pursuits

EPISODES IN
SOUTHERN
ART HISTORY

An Essay by

ESTILL CURTIS PENNINGTON

Within the study of American art, it is assumed that any work produced upon this continent by an artist from any background is subject to consideration. Within the realm of Southern art as a more specific, subjective study, this is not so. Thus, locating a body of Southern art is a complex matter, made more complex by the fact that a mere cataloging of objects does not constitute a study of Southern art. Once found, these objects must be interpreted within the body of prevailing thought; it is necessary to seek Southern themes in Southern art objects, which must be subjected to the same scrutiny that has been applied to other aspects of Southern studies.

ESTILL CURTIS PENNINGTON
Look Away: Reality and Sentiment in Southern Art

Introduction

In my volume *Look Away: Reality and Sentiment in Southern Art*, I sought to create a dialogue about the search for meaning in the painting of the South with a closely drawn distinction between the antiquarian and the connoisseur. Though tempered by criticism, I remain convinced that a matrix of antiquarians and connoisseurs–the former as a kind of cultural anthropologist seriously pre-occupied with the recovery of undocumented material culture and the latter as a prevailing interpreter of those objects–continues to provide the space where Southern art is hung.

Art appreciation is a rather cool, somewhat elite affair, reeking of the Appollonian impulse in Western civilization to categorize, to give order. Art history is the logical extension of the Appollonian desire to see things in an orderly progression. The antiquarian can calmly behold the art of the South, smile sweetly, and happily imagine that first came the itinerant portraitist and then the painters of swamp scenes.

Though perhaps a bit facile, this form of appreciation is altogether essential. It provides the very images which lead the connoisseur to question the values of a ruling planter class painted by portraitists of varying skills, even as they ponder the true meaning of those murky, forbidding swamps. "Art," writes the devastatingly brilliant Camille Paglia,"is order. But order is not necessarily just, kind, or beautiful."

To seek order is an antiquarian pursuit. All of us who are involved in the study of painting in the South should be deeply grateful to several particular antiquarians who salvaged and preserved much of the historical art which is extant. Together with the visionary artists and collectors of their day they ensured the survival of sufficient evidence for us to continue the critical sifting and cataloging which so concerns contemporary Southern studies.

What follows are six vignettes, meant to be terse and evocative, briefly stated but laden with further clues. Historical studies often come full circle. What the antiquarians have gathered, we now sort. It is time for our generation to pay homage, to gather and preserve, in proper bibliographic form, their writings and ephemera, even as we sigh in wistful longing for worlds as tidy as they imagined. Out of their alchemic elements gold may yet emerge from the dusty dross.

Estill Curtis Pennington

"No idle levity detracts from the solemnity of the occasion."

JAMES ROBB AND GEORGE COOKE INITIATE SOUTHERN COLLECTING

During the muggy, fetid spring of 1859, the wags and grandees of mongrel New Orleans gathered at the uptown residence of banker James Robb to witness the final act in the first elaborate pageant of Southern art collecting. Ambitious, self-made, and more than slightly defiant, Robb had met what seemed to be the classic Southern fate: come-uppance.

Upon the auction block his outstanding collection of European, American, and Southern painting was being sold off to the highest bidder in an effort to clear all outstanding debts. Although he had reached for the stars in the most lofty Victorian manner, Robb, in a moment of desperate need, demonstrated that he could indeed do the right thing. Inevitably time and tide have proven him to be both correct and worthy of extended interest.

James Robb was a man well-matched to the spirit and promise of New Orleans. Into the quiet backwater of a seemingly dignified colonial culture dominated by the whispers and cadences of émigré French provincials, the raucous American frontiersman had spilled with all the energy of a raging river at full flood tide. From crass Kentucky flatboatmen to ingenuous entrepreneurs, Americans from the western regions of the young republic poured South. Business and investment opportunities in New Orleans were not wasted upon Robb, a savvy banker from Wheeling, Virginia (now West Virginia).

From his first days as a cashier in a bank in Pittsburgh, Robb had worked his way up to a major position with one of several Northern banks which used the vantage point of river travel for speculation in western development. Biding his time, Robb looked South. By 1837 he had accumulated enough investment capital to move to New Orleans and begin his assault on a speculative center which the French denizens disparagingly referred to as "the American district."

He founded an important bank in partnership with several other individuals whom he quickly bought out, and with great foresight acquired the major portion of the first important utility concern in the South, the New Orleans Gas Light Company. "Thus by age twenty-nine," his most important contemporary biographer S. Frederick Starr has observed, "eight years after his arrival in New Orleans, Robb presided over both the burgeoning local utilities com-

JAMES ROBB AND
GEORGE COOKE
INITIATE SOUTHERN
COLLECTING

pany and his own bank."

At first Robb lived modestly in New Orleans, although, as Starr remarks, "there was nothing modest about Robb's taste in art, and his collection of old master and modern paintings grew with his fortune." As a collector Robb manifested an astuteness in the acquisition of fine art works which rivalled his carefully stewarded investment portfolio. Current locations of many art works he acquired reflect the regard in which they are now held. Hiram Powers' *Greek Slave* anchors the rotunda gallery of the Corcoran Gallery in Washington, D.C. His Asher Brown Durand, *September Forenoon*, may have been the first American luminist masterpiece in the South, inspiring the local Southern landscape school, and is now one of the finest works of its type held by the New Orleans Museum of Art.

Throughout the 1840s Robb collected with great enthusiasm. In 1845 he bought several works at the Jerome Bonaparte auction in Bordentown, New Jersey, where the defeated Emperor's brother had lived a sedate, rather elegant, exile. By 1852 these works, together with paintings by Leutze and Kellogg among the American artists, represented one of the most distinguished collections in America, and certainly in the South. A catalog raisonne of Robb's holdings would have extensive tentacles extending into major museum and private effects throughout this country today.

In 1844 Robb crossed paths with the Southern itinerant portrait artist George Cooke, an intersection at which the South's most esteemed collector met the South's most ardent champion for art awareness. Cooke earnestly desired to use his own paintings to "form the nucleus of a magnificent gallery" in New Orleans, according to an account penned by his brother at the time of the artist's early death. To that end he had been assisted by the patronage of the Alabama architect/industrialist Daniel Pratt.

Pratt provided Cooke with ample space on the third and fourth floors of a warehouse at #13 St. Charles Street. When Cooke's "National Gallery" opened there in 1844, the *Daily Picayune* for April 26 encouraged the public "to attend the fine display of originals and copies of celebrated Italian masters, to whose works the greater portion of our populace can never have access." Cooke's gallery was generously supported by loans of art works from the Robb Collection, including several from the Bonaparte sale.

Cooke himself had copied Raphael's *Transfiguration*, a painting he found "equally sublime, and composed with equal simplicity." His selection of the Raphael as a copy subject was motivated by a profound grasp of the Renais-

JAMES ROBB AND
GEORGE COOKE
INITIATE SOUTHERN
COLLECTING

sance master's spirituality. In a series of articles on the fine arts which Cooke penned for the *Southern Literary Messenger* in 1835, he exudes that the "whole scene rises before you with such propriety of expression in every countenance . . . no trifling ornamentation diverts attention from the subject . . . no idle levity detracts from the solemnity of the occasion."

Sadly enough, Cooke's often frantic efforts to create a public museum and support his own artistic career proved his undoing, and he died in 1849 in New Orleans from Asiatic cholera. Although Cooke's vision of an important art museum in the South would be postponed for another fifty years, Robb launched a personal building program of staggering proportion in 1851.

With the assistance of Richard Morris Smith, an architectural student of Thomas U. Walters, Robb began the construction of a luxurious Italiante palazzo in the Garden District, upriver from the French Quarter. Extensive gardens were laid out, terraces constructed, and interior murals commissioned from the local painter Domenico Canova.

Once complete, Robb installed his art collection, including the old masters, his portrait by Trevor Thomas Fowler, and the portrait of his wife and young children by Thomas Sully. But his occupancy was brief. A pyramidal collapse of the Cincinnati Insurance Company caused runs on Robb's banks in New York, San Francisco, and Liverpool. In short order he was $3,000,000 in debt.

But history, to turn a Victorian phrase, is often a cruel and ironic mistress. Robb liquidated his New Orleans properties before the War and left for the North, removing himself from the total collapse of Southern capital as a result of the internecine conflict. In later years he recovered his prosperity and lived contentedly with what was left of his collection in Cincinnati. His legacy was an inspiring passion for collecting, a beautiful building which became the first site of the Newcomb School of Art, and a personal example of great valor.

Like the handsome portrait of him which survives in the Historic New Orleans Collection, he was a brave and laughing cavalier who more than fostered the idea of art appreciation in the South. He led the way.

"Mary appeared so anxious to have my portrait taken that I could not decline gratifying her."

HAUNTING LIKENESSES OF ROBERT E. LEE

As the tiresome example of George Cooke illustrates, the life of the itinerant portraitist in the Old South was not always a pleasant, or even satisfying, one. Moving from town to town desperately seeking commissions often proved to be neither rewarding, nor especially stimulating to creativity. And yet the largest body of extant work from the period is portraiture. Circumstances surrounding the taking of a likeness provide many of the most fascinating episodes in the history of Southern art.

After all, truly important portraits come down the line enveloped in two-fold sagas: the story of the artist and the story of the sitter. This intersection, if you will, is the stuff of eventful sittings, that brief moment when the talented artist who has come to command our attention, chats briefly with the sitter, whose life is more fully illustrated by the likeness their meeting leaves behind.

It is little wonder then, that of all Southern sitters, Robert E. Lee has left behind the most appealing and highly evocative visual images. Lee sat for few life portraits. As a young man he was painted by the celebrated Kentucky artist William Edward West in Baltimore. Edward Caledon Bruce is thought to have sketched him from life in Richmond in 1865. Once in retirement at Lexington, he sat for Frank Buchser, a Swiss itinerant working in Reconstruction Virginia. And, as a very old man, he posed for the sculptor Edward Virginius Valentine.

General Lee was also captured in a fantasy historical setting of propitious moment by an artist whose raw talent and earnest ideals met in one monumental work. It is this portrait, E.B.D. Julio's *The Last Meeting of Lee and Jackson*, which endures as the most lasting picture of the gallant man in grey, astride a grey horse, dressed in a grey uniform and facing the grey arena of human conflict.

Lee's first portrait reminds us that he was not always grey. In March 1838, the young Robert E. Lee and his wife Mary Ann Randolph Custis Lee were making their way west where Lee was to continue his work with the Army Corps of Engineers at the clogged St. Louis passageway. Stopping in

HAUNTING LIKENESSES OF ROBERT E. LEE

Baltimore, Mrs. Lee determined to have her portrait painted, as well as Lee's. While legends surrounding the portraits have often mistaken them for wedding pictures, the Lees had, by that time, been married for almost seven years.

Mary Custis Lee's correspondence indicates she chose West, the reigning society portrait artist of the day, for "Robert, but as for me, I prefer Sully." Sully painted neither, but West did a fine job with both Lees. He had arrived in Baltimore late in 1837, flush with European artistic successes that included having painted Lord Byron, but completely bankrupt from foolish speculative ventures.

By all accounts, and the smashing body of work left behind, West was at the top of his form. From his origins as an itinerant on the Mississippi River, he had graduated to a world class portraitist in the romantic style. His style was warmly colored, placed the subject in close proximity to the picture plane, and flattered without caricature.

Subject and artist were well met. Lee was thirty years old, formidably handsome, and endowed with an endearing, engaging personality.

Montgomery C. Meigs, his future opponent, but contemporary companion, recalled that Lee, in 1837, "was in the vigor of youthful strength, with a noble and commanding presence, and an admirable, graceful and athletic figure." And so West depicted him. Lee's hair is windswept and side-brushed in the late Empire tradition. He wears the dress uniform Mrs. Custis had sent up "on the cars" from Arlington. His gaze, from the round and luminous brown eyes, is kindly and benign. He seems indeed "the beau ideal of the Christian gentleman," to quote again from Meigs.

When next we see the military hero in art, circumstances have changed. Though E.B.D. Julio did not paint the General from life, he did capture a riveting moment in time. Julio's work, composed in late 1869, depicts the last meeting of Lee and Jackson prior to the victorious battle of Chancellorsville when Confederate forces gained their last truly significant victory, even as Jackson perished in the effort.

Julio was neither Southern nor renowned when he undertook this effort. An emigrant artist of vaguely Italian origins, he had grown up on Napoleon's island of exile, St. Helena. By the time he began *The Last Meeting* in St. Louis, he had studied in Europe and Boston, operating as an artistic factotum, but one with high aspirations. He felt "perhaps through proper study I could proclaim myself the historical painter of the South. . . ."

More than he ever realized in his own lifetime, he was successful in that

HAUNTING LIKENESSES OF ROBERT E. LEE

aspiration. Although he drew the likeness of Lee and Jackson from available photographs and prints, the likenesses he created of the two Generals, heads together, astride their horses, are manifestations of uncanny accuracy. Lee himself, when solicited for his opinion, felt "the effect is spirited and the execution is good," though he declined Julio's offer to present him the enormous work as a gift.

With some desperation, Julio had transported the painting from St. Louis to New Orleans. From its arrival in 1870 until the artist's death in 1879, it was frequently on public display. In 1872 Julio had commissioned the engraver Halpin, of New York, to make a print for use in a lottery sale of the painting. Though the painting remained unsold, the print entered the popular imagination as the quintessential image of the Lost Cause.

And so they continue to sit. Two revered generals, on horseback, conferring with graceful gestures towards the battlefield, the subordinate with his head slightly inclined towards his commander-in-chief. Frustrated in life, Julio can surely rest in peace for sending Lee and Jackson towards eternity in an attitude of victory, even as the inevitability of defeat loomed.

Lee sat for a final likeness. Edward Virginius Valentine, scion of a great family of Richmond, Virginia philanthropists and antiquarians, journeyed to Lexington in June 1870, to make a portrait bust of the retired General. Lee was President of Washington College then, practicing in that role what he offered in his famous General Orders No. 9. "You will take with you the satisfaction that proceeds from the consciousness of duty faithfully performed," he told his battle-weary troops. As an educator Lee sought to mend the wounds of war, and create a new brand of Southern gentleman.

When Lee sat for Valentine for the sculpting of the portrait bust, he was in the final year of his life. Valentine found him "perfectly natural in his manners," despite all the adulation. "To have assumed a pose would not have been possible for him. He had a delightfully modulated voice, and a good deal of humor too." Valentine also found that Lee never spoke of the war. Rather, he reminisced "of earlier days when as a youth he used to go swimming in the Potomac at Alexandria."

Valentine's completed work provided the basis for his image of Lee in the famous recumbent, funereal pose. Lee rests upon his bier like a medieval warrior, who does not sleep but only rests until the final battle. In death, as in life, Lee inspired the artist and the generations to come.

"To each he gave the proper quality of its own time."

CHARLES HENRY HART DISCOVERS MATTHEW HARRIS JOUETT

In May 1899, *Harper's Magazine* published an article by Charles Henry Hart entitled "Kentucky's Master-Painter. Matthew Harris Jouett, 1788-1827." *Harper's* had frequently published articles by Hart, considered at that point the leading authority on historical American portraiture. But in this instance Hart departed from his more familiar subject matter—Gilbert Stuart and the Philadelphia portraitists—to generate interest in an ante-bellum Southern artist.

Jouett had hardly been an unknown quantity in his day. Following the path of fellow Kentuckian William Edward West, Jouett practiced an itinerancy up and down the Mississippi River from Lexington to Natchez to New Orleans and back, from 1817 until his untimely demise in 1827. His portraits were painted in a distinctly personal interpretation of Stuart's crisp neo-classical style. Jouett studied with Stuart in Boston—an experience he confided to a diary, the publication of which represents the most substantial body of information on Stuart's technique.

However, the only national assessment of Jouett's career had appeared in 1834 when William Dunlap, in his landmark *History of the Rise and Progress of the Arts of Design in the United States*, cited a letter from Henry Clay, Jr. The young Clay felt "Jouett was a man of taste and possessed a vein of humor copious and rich but unaffected and innocent in its tendency, which made him a charming companion, and which will perhaps add greatly to the interest of his biography."

Hart eventually reached a similar conclusion from his sincere, though somewhat suspect, regard for Jouett's portraiture. Written in the tone and tenor of the period, Hart, in a series of two articles on the old master of the Bluegrass, approaches Jouett with that slightly over-ripe antiquarian condescension which characterizes almost all Northern response to the culture of the South in the late nineteenth and early twentieth century.

Hart begins his article by marvelling that Jouett, as an artist of the "west," could have developed at all. "The conditions of soil and service," he opines, "would seem to leave neither opportunity nor possibility for the development of an art instinct." And yet Jouett emerges.

CHARLES HENRY HART DISCOVERS MATTHEW HARRIS JOUETT

Hart, a native Philadelphian of recent emigrant parents, seems to have had no knowledge of the cultural and economic achievements of the Old South as manifested in the Bluegrass state. Lexington was once called the "Athens of the West." The first libraries, universities, and theaters west of the Alleghenies were located in Jouett's hometown.

Yet Hart more than gracefully makes up for both his ignorance and condescension with an earnest amazement that the historical portraiture exhibition at the Philadelphia Centennial "should have failed to bring to the front a knowledge of Jouett's art." Hart, as the organizer of that exhibition, is being slyly self-critical even in the midst of self-aggrandizement. The Philadelphia Centennial is generally credited with having sparked the entire colonial revival in the decorative arts, together with a profoundly extensive interest in American portraiture.

To make amends, Hart did include Jouett in the Colombian Exposition exhibition on the same topic in Chicago in 1892-93. Jouett's sublimely cool portrait of John Grimes, now in the collection of the Metropolitan Museum of Art, may have been somewhat lost amidst the hundreds of American artworks. Still, it was the only Southern work of its type and period in the entire exhibition.

Hart's first article on Jouett established a skeletal outline for the artist's biography. His father's exploits as a kind of Southern Paul Revere, riding to Charlottesville warning the Virginia Legislature of impending British attack, is recounted. So is Jouett's early education at Transylvania University in Lexington, and his decision to become a painter despite training as a lawyer.

Hart was given access to numerous Jouett documents by descendants, including the famous notes on Gilbert Stuart on whom Hart had conducted extensive research. He generously allows that "Stuart's influence over Jouett seems to have had only the effect of giving added versatility to his methods of work." Indeed Hart found Jouett's works to be so "much like Stuart's that it is difficult to believe they are the production of any other hand."

Antiquarian in tone, the article seldom ventures beyond conclusions of a rather sentimental nature, such as his observations on Jouett's ability to depict the character of certain individuals. "To each he gave the proper quality of its own time. Helplessness, purity, vitality, strength, and decadence were delineated by him with equal power and truth."

Be that as it may, Hart does make some rather insightful comparative notes on the distinctions between the warm and cool "lights" in Jouett's work

CHARLES HENRY HART
DISCOVERS
MATTHEW HARRIS
JOUETT

and the "meretricious" use of color by contemporary impressionists. Like all good antiquarians, Hart had considerable disdain for the art of his own time.

Hart followed up his first article on Jouett a year later, with a piece entitled "Jouett's Kentucky Children," a work with a vaguely proto-formalist intent. Jouett's children's portraits are rather carefully analyzed as to composition and color, and interesting comparisons are made to the paintings of Van Dyke and Greuze. Hart praises Jouett's "close observation and facility of expression," praise which is well deserved.

As a matter of fact, Jouett's portraits of children or mothers with their children, represent some of the best works in his entire oeuvre. Like many Southern itinerants Jouett frequently employed certain recurring anatomical conventions which work well in his portraits of children. Placed in the lower right corner of the picture plane and seen in profile or turned just slightly contrapposto to the picture plane, they are quiet, tentative images of children who seem to have been just barely able to restrain themselves during the sitting.

As Hart concludes the second article, he draws certain conclusions which have echoes in the study of Southern painting. He thought Jouett was very fortunate not to have had "foreign influence and instruction" which might have spoiled him. Unknowingly Hart is alluding to that state of the natural genius much admired in contemporary self-taught art in the South. At the same time it reinforces the notion of certain unique qualities in Southern painting of the early nineteenth century, especially portraiture.

But most prophetically Hart goes on to wonder if "it is possible not to feel that there must have been in his day, west of the mountains, some good examples of the works of great painters with which he came in contact." There certainly were, as amply catalogued in the later writings of Edna Talbott Whitley. Not surprisingly, one of those works was a portrait of a member of the Mason/Brown family by Stuart, thought to have been the first work of its type west of the Alleghenies.

Sadly enough, Hart's motivation in bringing Jouett to the attention of the larger American public is suspect. At least one current scholar of American portraiture has written that Hart was a secret dealer bulwarking a market of his own creation. Furthermore, Jouett's diaries were entrusted to Hart by various descendants. These were never returned, nor have they subsequently been found, a great loss to Southern art historical scholarship. Still, Hart richly deserves at least a certain notoriety for his efforts in providing the first serious look at any Southern painter in the nineteenth century.

"She turned up information, often unexpectedly, like the tesserae of a lost mosaic."

ANNA WELLS RUTLEDGE DOCUMENTS THE EARLY ARTISTS OF CHARLESTON

In Charleston it may be said that the past has not so much slept as napped. From time to time in this century, some diligent—or merely curious—soul has tapped the Holy City on the shoulder. Waking like some dreamy princess, the cultural heritage of the place has then come alive in a series of gorgeous episodes. In the first quarter of the century, a combination of visiting contemporary artists, like Alfred Hutty and Pauline Palmer, joined forces with such native talent as Alice Smith and Dubose Heyward to spark the Charleston Renaissance. Their scholarly counterpart, Anna Wells Rutledge, was a tireless antiquarian who mapped the course of early Charleston art with an attention to delightful detail unmatched in any other Southern endeavor of its type.

Miss Rutledge was well suited to the task. The daughter of a distinguished old Battery family, she seems to have grown up with "a continuing family interest in such matters" as the miniatures of Charles Fraser and the pastels of Henrietta Johnston. John Morrill Bryan, in his introduction to the University of South Carolina reprint of her pivotal *Artists in the Life of Charleston,* has her pegged as a true antiquarian, with a fiercely historical spirit and an almost archeological regard for the flotsam and jetsam of biographical data. "She turned up information, often unexpectedly, like the tesserae of a lost mosaic."

Rutledge began to accumulate information on the subject of the artist in Charleston as early as 1928 when she was an apprentice, of sorts, to Laura M. Bragg of the Charleston Museum. When Bragg went to work at the Valentine Museum in Richmond, Miss Rutledge went with her. This experience of working in one of the great antiquarian libraries of the Old South surely set the tone for much subsequent research activity.

To some extent Anna Rutledge followed a well-known English pattern of antiquarian fact-finding. As far back as Horace Walpole in the eighteenth century, the English had carefully tucked away bits and pieces of curious lore in various collections and publications. When Rutledge quotes Walpole's self-effacing disclaimer from his *Anecdotes,* that "he pretended 'to no

ANNA WELLS RUTLEDGE DOCUMENTS THE EARLY ARTISTS OF CHARLESTON

more than specifying the professors of most vogue,' " the proper tone has been struck.

Artists in the Life of Charleston is organized as a tapestry of individual episodes drawn primarily from newspaper and secondary accounts in the period circa 1860 to 1865. From the outset her stated intentions were clearly in the antiquarian mode: to evoke the past with some certainty rather than re-create by some false interpretation. "I am glad to set this past on paper for it can never be reassembled in its entirety: even if partially re-collected it might well be a travesty of the original."

Following an historical introduction, in which the affinities between England and colonial South Carolina are firmly defined, Rutledge moves through the decades with a precision guided by the actual course of events and fleshed out with a careful, albeit wry, narrative explication of previous idiomatic expressions. "For two centuries," she felt, "South Carolina's life and thought followed the English archetype."

Archetypically, this resulted in a preference for portraiture as a visual art form, a conservative approach to new styles of art, and a lingering affection for the art of the past rather than contemporary expression. In this climate of taste, it is not unexpected that portraitists of long residence and visiting artists of acceptable renown flourished.

Due to its prosperity and considerable prominence as a seaport in eighteenth century America, Charleston had the most sophisticated culture south of New York and Boston. Henrietta Johnston and Mark Catesby worked in the area in the first quarter of the eighteenth century, more than sixty years before any recorded activity elsewhere in the Deep South.

Indeed, in many respects, the eighteenth century was the greatest period in Charleston's cultural history. At this time the portraitist Jeremiah Theus was busily painting his renditions of English court portraits as applied to the local gentry. However, Rutledge lists many other painters of lesser, and perhaps greater, ability who competed with Theus for commissions, creating the impression of a vital artistic community even as the state and nation moved towards and through the revolution.

In the area of nineteenth century studies, one of Rutledge's richest contributions is her establishment of the exact point of visitation by various itinerant artists working in Charleston. Samuel F.B. Morse, Gilbert Stuart, John Vanderlyn, John Wesley Jarvis, Thomas Sully, and George Cooke are all noted and tucked into their proper time frame. Recording the history of the

ANNA WELLS RUTLEDGE
DOCUMENTS
THE EARLY ARTISTS OF
CHARLESTON

South Carolina Art Academy disproves many Northern held theories on the absence of substantative cultural institutions in the ante-bellum South.

Continuing the account through the conclusion of the War Between the States, Rutledge is at pains to dispel, as well as prove. "It is possible that Jane Stuart . . . came to Charleston on a visit" but even if she did not, several portraits of George Washington "were her work." With equal honesty she documents the famous anecdote of G.P.A. Healey being asked to leave Charleston on the eve of the late unpleasantness due to his alleged Union sympathies. "Thus ended the generous welcome extended to Northern artists for over a century."

Following the historical narrative of the volume, the various appendixes are an exhaustive presentation of all actual facts regarding artists, objects, and art activities in Charleston, again, as gleaned from various published accounts. In many respects these annotations and lists are a remarkable achievement, rivalled in Southern studies only by the WPA artist project in New Orleans. But that account was assembled by several dozen paid researchers. Anna Wells Rutledge worked alone.

"Not having a purpose causes wrinkles in the soul."

EDNA TALBOTT WHITLEY WRITES *KENTUCKY ANTE-BELLUM PORTRAITURE*

Like the lively heroine of some late nineteenth century sentimental novels published in her native commonwealth, Edna Talbott Whitley was indeed "a girl of old Kentucky." She proudly numbered among her ancestors no less than fifteen veterans of the Revolutionary War, and throughout her life she was a stalwart member of the Jemima Johnson Chapter, Daughters of the American Revolution, which her mother had helped found in 1896.

However, the young Edna Talbott never thought of herself as a bluestocking from an aristocratic class. Instead she relentlessly researched the pioneer traditions of Kentucky, reading and indexing the earliest newspapers for evidence of patterns of settlement, family connections, and behavioral norms in an unsettled frontier society besieged by Indians and often shaken by either the fevers of religious fundamentalism or drunken excess on native Bourbon whiskey.

EDNA TALBOTT
WHITLEY WRITES
*KENTUCKY
ANTE-BELLUM
PORTRAITURE*

The results of her tenacious antiquarian activity may be seen in the articles she wrote for the *Kentucky Historical Register* and in her definitive studies of Kentucky cabinet-making and portraiture. *Kentucky Ante-Bellum Portraiture*, published in 1956, was the first exhaustive investigation of patterns of patronage and itinerancy in a critical area of painting in the South.

Mrs. Whitley was born in Paris, Bourbon County, Kentucky, one of the oldest settlements in the Bluegrass region. As a child she was educated locally in the genteel tradition of home schools, which stressed the reading of classics, the practice of music and dance, and the acquisition of a strong moral, spiritual, and intellectual discipline. By the time of Mrs. Whitley's birth, Bourbon County was old, settled, venerable, and resistant to change. The atmosphere in which she matured, married, and began her career as an amateur writer and antiquarian was certainly far removed from any great seat of learning, and yet she pursued a distinguished scholarly career.

Her motivation and persistence may have been derived in large part from the efforts of her mother. Sally Grimes Talbott not only inspired the local DAR to roll bandages for the Spanish-American War, she collected "antiques" as well. When she began rounding up various examples of Kentucky furniture for her own home on Duncan Avenue in Paris, the appreciation for "old things" was still a rather new concept. "She bought back furniture that had been given to servants and from relatives who wanted golden oak. She collected five sideboards, one for each of her children, and stored them in the stable and basement," Mrs. Whitley recalled in an interview with the *Lexington Herald Leader*, October 29, 1972.

Mrs. Whitley began her adult life as a housewife. Her husband, Wade Hampton Whitley, was a local attorney, and after his early death she taught piano and wrote various articles until the inspiration for a project on Kentucky portraiture sparked her scholarly endeavor.

In 1938 her friend and fellow Colonial Dame Katherine Stout Bradley of Georgetown, Kentucky, presented the Historical Activities Committee of the state organization with a scrapbook of photographs of portraits. These photographs provided the basis for a much needed and far more sweeping study of the subject.

In the preface of her volume, Mrs. Whitley summed up the advantages of the project in terms that continue to define the parameters of Southern portrait studies. Her goals were "threefold: the preservation of the known history of each painting, artist, portrait subject, which in the process of oral transmis-

EDNA TALBOTT
WHITLEY WRITES
KENTUCKY
ANTE-BELLUM
PORTRAITURE

sion, was in danger of becoming vaguer with successive generations; the preservation of photographs as insurance against complete loss, since most of the portraits were housed in private homes and thus subject to destruction by fire; the opportunity afforded for study of a number of works by known artists, at given periods of their productivity, as well as those of unknown painters who might be identified in the process." With this well-considered approach to artist, sitter, and object in mind, she began to collect portrait images.

To a large degree this process was facilitated by the Colonial Dames organization whose members tracked down objects and commissioned photographs. However, it quickly became apparent that very few of the portraitists themselves were identified, since works were seldom signed, and attributions were often a matter of oral history of a fanciful sort.

To identify the portrait artists, Mrs. Whitley turned to the Frick Art Reference Library in New York City. Several times a year she trekked north on the train from Paris, staying in the Barbizon Hotel for Women, walking the few blocks to Fifth Avenue, notebook in hand. Helen Clay Frick and J. Hall Pleasants of Baltimore had been collecting photographs of Southern portraits for more than twenty years, and these were carefully catalogued and housed in the library. Mrs. Whitley's appreciation for the Frick was unbounded. "Without the pioneer work done in Kentucky by that Foundation," she told Justus Bier, the distinguished art critic for the *Louisville Courier-Journal,* "I doubt if the book would have been undertaken."

Through the tedious method of verisimilitude of detail, Mrs. Whitley began to sort through the photographs, targeting signature aspects of compositional and anatomical detail, modelling, and contouring. As a result of this approach, and her lengthy readings in the literature of the period, she was able to define the work of more than 125 artists working in Kentucky.

Kentucky Ante-Bellum Portraiture is more than a family album of the Bluegrass elite. The book is organized by county, and each portrait found within each county is identified, when possible, by artist, with a complete biographical sketch of the sitter. Most importantly, at the back of the volume Mrs. Whitley published notes on 620 portrait artists working in the period, including those in Kentucky.

These sketches were gleaned from a variety of sources as disparate as brief newspaper advertisements to published autobiographies. All of these sources are recorded in the book's comprehensive bibliography, a work which rivals the exhaustive quality of her artists' sketches. Until a lengthy biograph-

EDNA TALBOTT
WHITLEY WRITES
KENTUCKY
ANTE-BELLUM
PORTRAITURE

ical dictionary of artists working in the South is published, those 200 pages will remain the conclusive reference on the subject. While certain artists, like Matthew Harris Jouett, William Edward West, and Oliver Fraser, were well known to her audience, many others, like Asa Park and Alexander Bradford, were not.

When the volume appeared it was well received by both the scholarly community and the lay antiquarian. Justus Bier praised the volume in a review published June 10, 1956 as "a monumental work. It is a documentation of the most important phase in the early art life of a state where portraiture for a long time overshadowed all other types of art."

Although severely injured in an automobile accident in the late 1940s that left her confined to a wheelchair for the rest of her life, Mrs. Whitley remained a vital, active scholar. She once joked that she would work in any court house "where someone would hand the books down to me." Her dedicated antiquarianism guaranteed the survival of critical scholarly material culture as well as the codification of extant records. But then she liked to stay busy. On her eighty-eighth birthday she commented that "not having a purpose causes wrinkles in the soul."

"Their pictures...became part of the cultural milieu of the South"

AMERICAN PAINTERS OF THE SOUTH OPENS AT THE CORCORAN

As the centennial of the War Between the States approached, many state and local historical societies and museums began to develop projects commemorating the anniversary. Obviously the vast majority of these projects evolved into special exhibitions with a focus upon military history. At the same time, the centennial sparked a new interest in the history of the South, particularly in critical Southern figures. Throughout the Southland itself, the reverberating waves of change brought about by the *Brown v. Board of Education* decision and the first victories of the civil rights movement prompted a new age of cultural examination.

AMERICAN PAINTERS OF THE SOUTH OPENS AT THE CORCORAN

Revisionism held much of the scholarly imagination in sway, with the result that the South was increasingly coming to be seen as neither quite so dreamy, nor quite so utterly wretched as the sharply divided proponents of each side had maintained. Still, much of this new spirit of investigation and analysis focused upon the social, political, and exonomic history of the South. Material culture was largely ignored, save by a few antiquarians. Gains were made in appreciation of Southern architecture and decorative arts, but Southern painting as a topic for scholarly study continued to languish.

The single most important exception to this trend was the exhibition *American Painters of the South* organized by the Corcoran Gallery of Art and held in Washington from April 23 to June 5, 1960. Both the site and the administration of the exhibition were highly appropriate. Washington was still, at that time, a very Southern city, redolent with tropical summer heat and humidity, inhabited by a largely white, Southern, indigenous population engrossed in the same ambiguous relationship with blacks that could be found in New Orleans or Richmond or Charleston.

The Corcoran itself was an institution with strong Southern ties. William Wilson Corcoran was a great friend of Robert E. Lee, often meeting Lee at the old Greenbrier resort at White Sulphur Springs during Lee's last days. Corcoran's personal collection included John Adams Elder's portraits of Robert E. Lee and Stonewall Jackson, which he gave to the museum in 1884.

Herman Warner Williams, director of the Corcoran, was a noted specialist in the art of the War Between the States, and frequently voiced a sincere interest in the painting of the South. Apart from Corcoran's gift, the museum held many excellent examples of works by Southern painters, and these formed the basis of the exhibition.

From the outset one of the most meaningful historiographical achievements of the exhibition as conceived and organized sprang from the very definition of the South. In her terse yet insightful introduction, Eleanor Swenson Quandt defined a geographic range "from Maryland and Missouri on the North to the Carolinas and Louisiana on the South."

This reference to the Northern border of the South as established by the Mason-Dixon Line must always be affirmed as the cartographic division between Maryland and Pennsylvania. Maryland, Kentucky, and Missouri, while border states, were shaped by Southern agrarian values, and challenged by the politics of slavery and secession. The first painters in those areas were patronized by the Southern planter class, especially the portraitists.

AMERICAN PAINTERS
OF THE SOUTH
OPENS AT
THE CORCORAN

Quandt and all subsequent Southern art historians have recognized the need to consider the works of non-indigenous artists working alongside local talent for comparative critical reasons. Speaking of the non-indigenous artist, Quandt writes, "their pictures, however, became a part of the cultural milieu of the South and inevitably influenced indigenous developments." These influences were most apparent in the area of portraiture, which tends to respond very strongly to popular stylistic trends and successful market indicators.

Restricting the exhibition to an area defined in the Deep South by South Carolina and Louisiana reflects the strongly eighteenth and early-to-mid-nineteenth century flavor of the exhibition. As Quandt herself points out, the work of Anna Wells Rutledge on the Charleston painters and Perry T. Rathbone on the lower Mississippi Valley artists had become classics in their field. Whether by intent or pleasant circumstance, the exhibition truly represented the spirit, in genre art and portraiture, of the Old South.

Many of the artists chosen for the exhibition continue to be regarded as having provided cornerstone material culture for Southern painting studies. While the inclusion of colonial itinerants like Wollaston, Hesselius, and Bridges was predictable enough, the discovery and wider showing of artists like Jeremiah Theus, Henrietta Johnston, and George Beck moved the exhibition beyond one of mere antiquarian concern.

It is particularly significant that the Peales were included. Though often associated with Philadelphia, it should be remembered that their origins were in rural Maryland and their first successes in Baltimore. Rembrandt Peale was more responsible for the cult of George Washington than any other artist of his day, and the emerging Southern nationalists laid claim to him with considerable fervor.

By including Boqueta di Woiseri and Richard Clague, the Corcoran gave public showings to Deep South artists whose works had seldom been seen outside their native regions. Clague was included in *Mississippi Panorama* but had no profile as an atmospheric luminist beyond New Orleans. His steamy, humid depictions of the Louisiana landscape synthesized certain prevailing French Barbizon trends with a native response to the peculiar light qualities of Louisiana. As a body of work, Clague's paintings are among the most expressive evocations of that exotic terrain.

Omitted from the recent *Painting in the South* exhibition, George Caleb Bingham was included in the Corcoran scheme. Consideration of Bingham's

AMERICAN PAINTERS
OF THE SOUTH
OPENS AT
THE CORCORAN

work is essential to a fuller understanding of diverse currents of Southern style. While Bingham's subject matter can be considered to have a Western thrust, his energetic creations of jolly flatboatmen are completely bound up in a basic Southern folk type. Being Southern should be no more a matter of belief and stand on slavery than a matter of race. Complexity of cultural origin and patterns of association are of far greater importance. These the Corcoran recognized.

Of the romantic portraitists included in the exhibition, William Edward West emerged as the greatest rediscovery. By 1960 West's achievements as the painter of Lord Byron and Robert E. Lee had all but been forgotten. He was represented in the Corcoran show by two paintings, the coyly seductive painting of Ellen Ward Gilmore and the jolly baroque allegory of the Caton sisters as the three muses of painting, poetry, and music.

Finally, the most subtle work in the entire exhibition may have been Frank Blackwell Mayer's *Leisure and Labor*. In that painting we see one young man hard at work shoeing a horse, while another stands idly by, dressed in the cavalier manner of a Southern planter about to join the hunt. This diversity of activity and pose more than adequately defines the polarities of the Southern social setting as seen in genre painting.

Although relatively small and with only a modest catalog, the Corcoran exhibition on American painters in the South was a superb beginning for Southern art history. As Eleanor Quandt pointed out, the effort was intended to "supply additional raw material" for further study. The numbers of monographs, articles, and exhibitions on the individuals and period featured in the exhibition more than justify her hopes. From quaint beginnings as a subject for study by antiquarians searching for curious remnants of a dusty past, the study of Southern painting has moved slowly towards the full and often relentless light of objective connoisseurship.

Select Bibliography

American Painters of the South. Washington, D.C.: Corcoran Museum of Art, 1960.

Banks, William Nathaniel. "George Cooke and Daniel Pratt: An Improbable Friendship." In *George Cooke 1793-1849*, edited by Donald D. Keyes. Athens, Georgia: Georgia Museum of Art, 1991.

———."George Cooke, Painter of the American Scene," *The Magazine Antiques* CII (September 1972).

Bonner, Judith H. "Artists' Associations in Nineteenth Century New Orleans: 1842-1860," *The Southern Quarterly* (Fall & Winter 1985).

Cooke, Charles. *Descriptive Catalog of Paintings in the Gallery of Daniel Pratt, Prattville, Alabama, together with a memoir of George Cooke, Artist.* Prattville, Alabama, 1853.

Hart, Charles Henry. *Catalog of the Engraved Portraits of Washington*. New York, 1904.

———. *Frauds in Historical Portraiture*. Washington, D.C., 1915.

———. "Jouett's Kentucky Children," *Harper's Magazine* 101 (1900).

———. "Kentucky's Master-Painter, Matthew Harris Jouett, 1788-1827," *Harper's Magazine* 98 (1899).

———. *Portraits of Patrick Henry*. Philadelphia, 1913.

Keyes, Donald, ed. *George Cooke 1793-1849*. Athens, Georgia: Georgia Museum of Art, 1991.

Meredith, Roy. *The Face of Robert E. Lee in Life and Legend*. New York: Charles Scribner's Sons, 1947.

Pennington, Estill Curtis. "The Kentucky-Mississippi Itinerancy: West, Jouett, Bush and Lambdin," *The Southern Quarterly* 25 (Fall 1986).

———. *The Last Meeting's Lost Cause*. Spartanburg, South Carolina: Robert M. Hicklin Jr., Inc., 1988.

———. "Time in Travelling: Intimations of the Itinerancy of George Cooke." In *George Cooke 1793-1849*, edited by Donald Keyes. Athens, Georgia: Georgia Museum of Art, 1991.

Rudolph, Marilou A. "George Cooke and his Paintings," *Georgia Historical Society Quarterly* 44 (June 1960).

Rutledge, Anna Wells. "After the Cloth was Removed," *Winterthur Portfolio* 4 (1968).

——. *Artists in the Life of Charleston Through Colony and State from Restoration to Reconstruction*. Philadelphia: American Philosophical Society, 1949.

——."Charleston's First Artistic Couple," *The Magazine Antiques* 52 (August 1947).

——."Cogdell and Mills, Charleston Sculptors," *The Magazine Antiques* 41 (March 1942).

——."Handlist of Miniatures in the Collection of the Maryland Historical Society," *Maryland Historical Magazine* 40 (June 1945).

——."Paintings in the Council Chamber of Charleston City Hall," *The Magazine Antiques* 98 (November 1970).

——. "Who Was Henrietta Johnston?" *The Magazine Antiques* 51 (March 1947).

Simmons, Linda Crocker. "Chronological Survey: The Life of George Cooke." In *George Cooke 1793-1849*, edited by Donald D. Keyes. Athens, Georgia: Georgia Museum of Art, 1991.

Starr, S. Frederick. *Southern Comfort, The Garden District of New Orleans, 1800-1900*. Boston: MIT Press, 1989.

Stern, Philip Van Doren. *Robert E. Lee, The Man and the Soldier, A Pictorial Biography*. New York: McGraw-Hill Book Company, Inc., 1963.

Whitley, Edna Talbott. *Checklist of Kentucky Cabinetmakers from 1775 to 1859 with addendum*. Paris, Kentucky: 1969. Reprint, 1982.

——."George Beck, an 18th century painter," *Kentucky Historical Society Register* (January 1969).

——. *Kentucky Ante-Bellum Portraiture*. Richmond, Virginia: National Society of Colonial Dames in America in the Commonwealth of Kentucky, 1956.

——."Mary Beck and the Female Mind," *Kentucky Historical Society Register* (Winter 1979).

Acknowledgements

I am grateful to Mr. Hicklin and his staff, in particular gallery director Kim Tuck, project coordinator Holly Watters and editor Lynne Blackman, for their ongoing support of my scholarship and writing in the field of Southern art. As ever, the Fine Art Library of the Smithsonian Institution at the National Museum of American Art is a comforting refuge and endless help. This effort was also furthered by the research holdings of the Lauren Rogers Museum of Art in Laurel, Mississippi, and by the aid of its director, Mary Ann Pennington. Frank and Elizabeth Grimes Danforth were most generous with the family albums of Edna Talbott Whitley. Additional materials on James Robb were found in the extensive archival holdings of the Historic New Orleans Collection. But in the larger sense I must thank Mr. William S. Morris III for providing that shelter for Southern art studies which enables me to continue my pursuit.

Estill Curtis Pennington

Southern Art

from the holdings of

ROBERT M. HICKLIN JR., INC.

*in celebration of
the gallery's
twentieth anniversary*

All catalog entries written by
Estill Curtis Pennington;
with the exception of notes
on the portrait entitled
General James Edward Oglethorpe,
Founder of Georgia,
written by Philip Mould;
and notes on the artist
William Aiken Walker,
written by Cynthia Seibels.

UNKNOWN

General James Edward Oglethorpe, Founder of Georgia

Oil on canvas
30 1/4 x 25 1/4 inches
Circa 1745

PROVENANCE:
English collection until 1990

Born into a British family with strong Jacobite sympathies, James Edward Oglethorpe (1696-1785) was educated at Eton and Corpus Christi College, Oxford. He served in the army before going briefly to Europe to join the exiled Stuart royal family. Upon returning to England he took over the family estates in Surrey and in 1722 became a member of the British Parliament.

In Parliament his moralistic and philanthropic bent soon became clear. He opposed extravagance and debauchery in all forms. He served as chairman of a parliamentary committee on debtors' prisons and soon afterwards in 1732 he obtained a charter for the establishment of the "Colony of Georgia." He believed that the new colony would partly serve the purpose of relieving unemployment at home, particularly among newly freed debtors. He also saw it serving as a defensive zone between more established imperial and Spanish territories, and as a means of increasing trade and navigation.

Oglethorpe successfully negotiated with the native Indians for the site of Savannah and induced the Indians to end communications with the French and Spanish. Much of his time, however, was pre-occupied with military matters, in particular, colonial defense against Spanish invasion. Despite a lack of support from England which often forced Oglethorpe to use his personal finances, he was largely successful as a military leader. His failed attack on St. Augustine in 1743, however, marked the end of his career in Georgia and he subsequently returned to England, leaving behind a firmly established colony whose future success was assured.

The authorship of this portrait, like so many of this date, is uncertain. It appears to be an artist working close to the circle of William Aikman (1682-1731). The basis for its identity is the existence of a second version, inferior in quality but ascribable to the same hand, located at Oglethorpe University. It is illustrated in John Kerslake's *Early Georgian Portraits* published by the English National Portrait Gallery in 1977 and appears as the cover of *Early Georgia Portraits* published by the National Society of the Colonial Dames of America in 1975.

The gruff characterization illustrated here marks the onset of a more individualistic style in British portraiture which can be seen coming to fruition in the works of Sir Joshua Reynolds (1723-1792). There is a distinct departure from the more regulated, passive appearance of the earlier Augustan images of Kneller and his contemporaries, and as such belongs to the transitional style of eighteenth century British portraiture.

Paintings of Oglethorpe are particularly uncommon and the recent emergence of this prime version is of considerable significance in the context of Anglo-American iconography.

CHARLES PEALE POLK (1767-1822)

Born, Annapolis, Maryland; studied with his uncle, the painter Charles Willson Peale, 1778-1785; active as an itinerant in western Maryland and northern Virginia, 1796-1801; and in Baltimore and Washington, D.C. throughout his career; died, Mt. Pleasant, Virginia.

Portrait of Thomas Jefferson

Oil on canvas
27 1/4 x 24 inches
November 1799

PROVENANCE:
Victor Spark, New York, New York until 1990

LITERATURE:
Alfred L. Bush, *The Life Portraits of Thomas Jefferson* (Charlottesville, Virginia: Thomas Jefferson Memorial Foundation, Inc., 1987), 34 (reproduced).

Estill Curtis Pennington, *Look Away: Reality and Sentiment in Southern Art* (Spartanburg, South Carolina: Saraland Press, 1989), 14 (reproduced).

Linda Crocker Simmons, *Charles Peale Polk: A Limner and His Likenesses* (Washington, D.C.: Corcoran Gallery of Art, 1981), ii, 66 (reproduced).

Linda Crocker Simmons, "The Emerging Nation, 1790 to 1830," in *Painting in the South: 1564-1980*, ed. Ella-Prince Knox and David S. Bundy (Richmond, Virginia: Virginia Museum, 1983), 52, 199 (reproduced).

P olk's training with his uncle, the legendary colonial portraitist, would have acquainted him with certain well-developed artistic theories passed on directly from Benjamin West. This heritage and the persistent imaginative strain in the extended Peale family accounts, in part, for the artist's rather appealing body of work.

But Peale's background gives only a partial index of the style he brought to his portrait of Thomas Jefferson, the esteemed squire of Monticello. Jefferson was not an easy subject to capture, nor did he suffer portraitists gladly. And, while the Peale family seemed to have limitless access to Washington through the offices of Charles Wilson Peale's revolutionary war associates, the sage of Monticello was another matter.

Polk went about securing an introduction to Jefferson in the most time honored and tested Southern manner–the network of genteel and inter-related family connections. While working as an early itinerant artist in the valley of Virginia and in western Maryland, he had painted members of the Madison and Hite clans. James Madison, the future president, wrote a letter of introduction for the artist. Madison quite modestly informs Jefferson that Polk "visits Monticello with a wish to be favored with a few hours sitting for his pencil."

Once Jefferson granted this wish the result was one of the finest portraits in the canon of late eighteenth century Southern art, and surely Polk's masterpiece. Devoid of pretentious background detail and alive with the brooding vibrant soul of the greatest president, it is a subtle essay in character. Linda Simmons, in her definitive study of Polk, felt the artist "produced, in free and broadly brushed paint strokes, what may be characterized as the 'essential' Republican portrait." Above all else, Simmons writes, "the freshly painted, strongly brushed face is endowed with the spark of animation. . . ."

Ironically enough, Polk's portrait of Jefferson was painted at the close of the most active period of his career. After 1800 he became a minor clerk in the Federal government, and his painting commissions devolved upon the small, *verre églomisé* profile technique. Not long before his death he retired to rural Virginia, living precisely that idyllic existence, close to the earth, which Jefferson so admired.

JOHN ABBOT
(1751 - circa 1840)

Born, London, England; received instruction in England from Jacob Bonneau; active in Georgia, in the vicinity of Augusta, 1775-1779; and along the Ogeechee-Savannah River Basin, 1779-1840; died, Bulloch County, Georgia.

A Set of Drawings of Georgia Birds

Eighty watercolors on paper (See illustration of one, entitled "Pileated Woodpecker." Inscribed on verso: Pileated woodpecker. Picus Pileatus.) Each approximately 10 3/4 x 6 3/4 inches. 1824-26

EXHIBITIONS:
Swan Coach House Gallery, Atlanta, Georgia, *An Exhibition of a Collection of Watercolor Drawings Depicting Georgia Birds and Butterflies*, 1991.

LITERATURE:
This collection is the subject of an unpublished essay by Vivian Rogers-Price, Ph.D. entitled "John Abbot and His Birds of Georgia." Rogers-Price is the author of *John Abbot in Georgia: The Vision of a Naturalist Artist* (Madison, Georgia: Madison-Morgan Cultural Center, 1983), and co-author with William W. Griffin of "John Abbot: Pioneer-Naturalist of Georgia," *The Magazine Antiques*, October 1983, 768-775.

This collection of watercolors should be considered complete. The set is unbound, but the paper boards with ribbon ties which contained it are preserved. The collection is presented as eighty individual sheets, forty framed, with forty offered in five volumes of eight.

Each watercolor bears an inscription at the bottom which identifies the common name of the bird pictured, although on several sheets this information has been lost. In addition, there are inscriptions on the verso of each sheet which assign, when known, a scientific name, the dimensions of the bird, and if relevant the name of the butterfly species. All inscriptions are in Abbot's hand.

Each sheet of paper has suffered an elliptical cut along its lower margin. This cut removed a portion of the sheet which had apparently been damaged by mildew, proximity to a heat source, or some other misfortune. In the majority of cases this cut does not affect the image. In other instances, images are slightly affected and on two sheets, the cuts are erratic. Our paper conservator, using the most delicate of hands, has lightly cleaned each sheet. The two pages with more radical loss have had paper restored, though in no case has any image been enhanced. Each sheet has been hinged to another piece of period paper so that the inscription on the verso can be read.

Photographs of all subjects, a comprehensive description, and a list with common and scientific names are available. The collection is offered in its entirety. We would be pleased to see it join the ranks of whole volumes of birds such as those found at the British Museum of Natural History, Houghton Library at Harvard University, Hargrett Rare Books and Manuscripts Library at the University of Georgia, the Smithsonian Institution, and Lord Derby's Library, Knowsley Hall, Prescott, England. A single volume currently in private hands and this collection make the census of known major sets that are complete.

During his youth in London, Abbot was trained by the engraver and drawing master Jacob Bonneau. Bonneau's early influence is evident in Abbot's superb grasp of perspective and bent for meticulous detail. The naturalist's skill in watercolor, however, was apparently self-taught. These watercolors form the bulk of Abbot's oeuvre, though of the five thousand completed during his lifetime, less than two hundred were published. An introspective, unassuming man whose thoughts were "ingrossed [sic] by Natural history," Abbot's contributions to entomology, ornithology, and botany are today considered on par with those of his more famous contemporaries William Bartram and John James Audubon.

Pileated Woodpecker.

THOMAS ADDISON RICHARDS (1820-1900)

Born, London, England; active in Penfield, Augusta, and Athens, Georgia; and in Charleston, South Carolina, 1838-1845; made frequent trips to the South collecting materials for travel writing and illustration, 1845-circa 1870; died, Annapolis, Maryland.

The Nacoochee Valley, Georgia

Oil on paper
10 1/2 x 15 inches
Signed illegibly lower left
Circa 1842

PROVENANCE:
Private collection, Washington, Georgia until 1990

EXHIBITIONS:
Atlanta Historical Society, Atlanta, Georgia, *Land of Our Own, 250 Years of Landscape and Gardening Tradition in Georgia 1733-1983*, 1983.

Richard's fondness for this area in the north Georgia mountain country was undoubtedly nurtured by early years spent near Penfield, Georgia, where his father was principal of a very fine school. In his travel writings and sketches Richards often mentions Nacoochee as one of the most beautiful spots in the South.

Indeed those very writings are critical to an understanding of Richards' art. Unlike many of his contemporaries Richards was quite expressive about his particular views concerning landscape art. He created a large volume of published materials which offer specific insights on both locale and motivation. In his pivotal article, "The Landscape of the South," published in *Harper's Magazine* in 1853, Richards, as artist/journalist issues a clarion call to action on the Southern setting. "Little has yet been said, either in picture or story, of the natural scenery of the Southern States, so inadequately is its beauty known abroad or appreciated at home."

Paintings like the one at hand serve to remedy that situation in their sensitive combination of prevailing Hudson River School light techniques applied to a site-specific Southern locale. The Nacoochee mound was admired as a pre-historic Indian site even as the mountain pass was considered to be amongst the most picturesque in the Southern highlands.

HARRIETT CANY PEALE (1800-1869)

Born, Philadelphia; studied with Rembrandt Peale, whom she married in 1840; and at the Pennsylvania Academy of Fine Arts; died, Philadelphia.

Her Mistress's Clothes

Oil on panel
10 1/8 x 8 1/4 inches
Signed and dated lower right: HC Peale 1848

PROVENANCE:

Maxwell Galleries, San Francisco, California; Bernard Danenberg Galleries, New York; Mr. and Mrs. George J. Arden, New York until 1991

Despite their position in progressive Philadelphia society, the Peales were a Maryland family with a deeply Southern heritage. Their awareness of the role of slaves in Maryland and the tidewater South certainly flavors Harriet Peale's provocatively alluring depiction of social cross-dressing.

Approaching this picture from the adjusted viewpoint of social history, one understands the characterization best described by Guy McElroy in his volume *Facing History: The Black Image in American Art*. Without exception McElroy asserts, the "American genre tradition of depicting black people as comic stereotypes . . . continued uninterrupted until the outbreak of civil war."

Stereotypes cannot be denied in this unsettling work which does lend itself to a more expansive interpretation. Consider the painting as a visual manifestation of Ovidian metamorphosis, that process by which elements in the natural order are transformed for reflective purposes. According to Camille Paglia, Ovid's "world becomes a projected psyche, played upon by amoral vagaries."

So we see here, when the blank slate of the slave woman's life becomes the subject of her mistress's projection. In the process of cross-dressing, roles are altered and attitudes adjusted. The slave becomes far more striking, and the mistress takes on a certain benign, though somewhat condescending, air. More than polemic, this is a work of crafty insight into the subtle power and play of hieratic appearance.

35

THOMAS WIGHTMAN (1811-1888)

Born, Charleston, South Carolina; studied in New York with Henry Inman at the National Academy of Design, circa 1835; active in Charleston intermittently, 1841-1865; died, Charleston.

Tabletop Bounty
Oil on canvas
25 x 30 inches
Circa 1850

Wightman's training with Inman is more than apparent in the portrait style he employed upon his return to Charleston in the early 1840s. Inman was a master of the American grand manner image most popularly associated with the lush, elegant works of the Empire period (circa 1835-1850). In that same vein, Wightman's portraits have a great calming presence, defining the sitter in dignified and altogether proper terms.

However, during his period of study in New York Wightman was almost certainly exposed to certain emerging patterns in still life painting that altered the restrained juxtapositions of neo-classicism. After 1840 still life art in this country, responding to certain international trends, became much more busy and abundant in detail. The sprawling tendrils of coiling vines conveys the powerful mood of a people of plenty, very much in keeping with the national spirit.

The delicately spiraling lemon peel adds a delightfully provocative note, defying the picture plane and reaching out with a trompe l'oeil realism. This same motif is to be found in a similar work now in the possession of the Greenville County (South Carolina) Museum of Art.

Thomas Wightman's brother William was also a still life artist whose works are represented in the Gibbes Gallery in Charleston, South Carolina. The brothers almost certainly shared techniques and styles.

EDWARD BEYER
(1820-1865)

Born, Rhineland of Germany; studied at the Dusseldorf Academy; active in the South, in Virginia, 1854-1856; died Munich, Germany.

Lewisburg, Virginia

Oil on canvas
26 1/4 x 48 inches
Signed and dated lower right:
Ed. Beyer 1854

PROVENANCE:
Daniel Hart Stalanker to his daughter; Ellen Stalanker to her daughter; Rose Armstrong to her son, J.S. Dawson, Washington, D.C. until 1986

EXHIBITIONS:
Robert M. Hicklin Jr., Inc., Spartanburg, South Carolina; Phillips, New York; Swan Coach House Gallery, Atlanta, Georgia; Eaton Gallery, Memphis, Tennessee; Washington County Museum of Fine Arts, Hagerstown, Maryland: *Look Away: Reality and Sentiment in Southern Art*, 1987-1988.

LITERATURE:
Estill Curtis Pennington, *Look Away: Reality and Sentiment in Southern Art* (Spartanburg, South Carolina: Saraland Press, 1989), 45 (reproduced).

RELATED LITERATURE:
R. Lewis Wright, "Edward Beyer in America," *Art and Antiques*, November/December 1980, 73-77.

Beyer was one of a number of German artists who sought refuge in this country during the hectic days following the revolutionary year of 1848. He initially settled in the mid-Atlantic area, working in Newark and Philadelphia. Following the creation of a large panorama, painted in conjunction with the French artist Leo Elliott, he worked briefly in Cincinnati.

To that point Beyer was primarily involved in creating works of art grounded in his formal training, paintings intended to appeal to an audience likely to aid in his support. However, in 1854 the artist and his wife, perhaps for reasons of health, began to spend time amongst the celebrated healing springs of Virginia. Once there Beyer found the greatest outlet for his brush, rendering a series of highly detailed and impressive views, many of which were gathered in a publication, *Album of Virginia*, first issued in 1857.

From the apparent evidence of Beyer's visual art, his aesthetic is another manifestation of incipient German Romanticism as practiced by Joseph Anton Koch and Carl Rottman. Two currents of that bold, dramatic style are to be seen in this image of Lewisburg, Virginia—a cold, clear, realistic light enlivening a highly keyed coloration, and a subtle dissecting eye with a realist agenda.

THOMAS WATERMAN WOOD (1823-1903)

Born, Montpelier, Vermont; studied in Boston with Chester Harding; active in the South at Baltimore, 1856; Nashville, Tennessee, 1859-1861; and in Louisville, Kentucky, 1862-1865; died, Montpelier.

The Apple Vendor

Oil on canvas
18 1/2 x 14 1/2 inches
Signed and dated lower right: T.W. Wood. 1858

EXHIBITIONS:
Wunderlich & Co., Inc., New York, *For the Collector: Selected American Paintings of the 19th and 20th Centuries*, 1986, no. 3.
Greenville County Museum of Art, Greenville, South Carolina, *Art for Greenville*, 1986.

LITERATURE:
Cynthia Seibels, *For the Collector: Selected American Paintings of the 19th and 20th Centuries* (New York: Wunderlich & Co., Inc., 1986), 6 (reproduced).

This painting will be included in Paul Worman's forthcoming book on the artist's work.

Wood actually began his career as an itinerant portrait artist working up and down the Eastern Seaboard from New England to Baltimore. While in Baltimore in the immediate ante-bellum period he began to paint scenes from black life, notably the commercial ventures of freedmen working on the streets there. Baltimore had a large population of free and slave blacks, and like William Aiken Walker, Wood responded artistically to their various activities.

Wood's most consistent client in Baltimore was John C. Brune, for whom Wood is known to have painted a number of portraits and genre works. In the annals of Wood's accounts of his paintings, several genre works based on Baltimore subjects are listed. Speculation on this work has always concerned its association with a well-known street vendor named Hindoo John who indeed may be represented here.

Further speculation by Cynthia Seibels notes that the apple vendor at hand is a free man of color. Depictions of freedmen in the ante-bellum South were quite rare, compounding the historical note of the painting. Considering the poise, attire, and mood of the work, the freedman attribution seems highly likely. Though impressed by black subject matter Wood never turns to coarse or lampooning caricature, instead depicting the black figure with the kind of dignity and elan one associates with the Barbizon school of social naturalism.

41

JOHN J. PORTER
(1825 - circa 1860)

Born, Culpepper County, Virginia and active there throughout his life and career.

The Culpepper Hunt

Oil on canvas
16 1/8 x 30 1/8 inches
Circa 1858

PROVENANCE:
Jameson-LaRue Family, Culpepper County, Virginia; Frank Horton, Winston-Salem, North Carolina until 1988

John J. Porter seems to have been a very gifted, albeit self-taught, artist who worked in the upper valley of Virginia during the immediate ante-bellum period. His work is best known through the inter-related possessions of the Jameson-LaRue families of Culpepper County, Virginia.

Porter's work and the event he depicts were inspired by those English antecedents which Virginians loved– and continue to love. The ritualistic hunting of foxes on horseback is a lingering symbol of the placid affections of an established country gentry. In composition and mood Porter demonstrates a familiarity with certain English sporting prints of the late eighteenth century, especially in his long, attenuated forms, and the striking horizontal orientation of the picture plane.

EXHIBITIONS:
Robert M. Hicklin Jr., Inc., Spartanburg, South Carolina; Thomasville Cultural Center, Thomasville, Georgia; Swan Coach House Gallery, Atlanta, Georgia: *At Break of Dawn: Sporting Art in the South*, 1989-1990.

JOACHIN FERDINAND RICHARDT (1819-1895)

Born, Brede dei Lyngby, Denmark; studied at the Royal Academy, Copenhagen; active in the South, circa 1856-1873; died, San Francisco.

View of Harper's Ferry

Oil on canvas
28 1/2 x 48 1/2 inches
Signed lower left:
Ferd. Richardt
1858

PROVENANCE:
Kennedy Galleries, New York, New York; Senator and Mrs. John D. Rockefeller IV, Washington, D.C. until 1989

EXHIBITIONS:
Possibly included at National Academy of Design, New York, *Exhibition of American Scenery*, 1859.

LITERATURE:
Henry W. Bragdon, Samuel P. McCutchen, and Donald A. Ritchie, *History of A Free Nation* (Westerville, Ohio: Glencoe Division of Macmillan/McGraw-Hill School Publishing Company, 1992), 421 (reproduced).

"In Search of the Picturesque," *The Kennedy Quarterly* VI, no. 1 (April 1966): 15. Incorrectly identified as *Susquehanna River* (reproduced).

New York Herald, January 11, 1859.

Jean Woods, "Richardt captures scenic America on canvas," Hagerstown, Maryland *Herald-Mail*, Sunday, 16 December 1990, section E.

Crystalline clarity, a diffuse but illuminating light, and a highly developed sense of design are precisely the characteristics one would associate with the European training of Danish-born artist Ferdinand Richardt. As an artist/naturalist he was attracted by the special features of several major American bits of scenic wonder, including Niagara Falls, the Mammoth Cave of Kentucky, and the Natural Bridge of Virginia.

Harper's Ferry provided Richardt with one of his richest subjects. Dramatically located at the confluence of the Potomac and Shenandoah rivers, the little town occupies a prospect of spectacular views heightened by rush of water and soaring mountain passes. Richardt's view only slightly precedes the most famous episode in the history of Harper's Ferry. On October 16, 1859, the radical abolitionist John Brown attempted to spark a slave revolt by seizing the important Federal arsenal located near the town's point into the rivers.

Defeated by Robert E. Lee and J.E.B. Stuart, Brown was imprisoned under the gaze of Thomas J. "Stonewall" Jackson and tried by a jury pursuing the persecutory orders of Secretary of War Jefferson Davis. Thus in one brief moment did several major players in the Southern drama gather in the small town so beautifully painted by an itinerant artist of superb ability.

RUDOLPH T. LUX (1815-1868)

Born, Germany; active in New Orleans, 1856-1868; died, New Orleans.

Portrait of Judah P. Benjamin

Gilt & polychrome enamel on porcelain
7 1/4 inches in diameter
Inscribed on verso:
"Painted & Gilded/By/Rudolph T. Lux/N. Orleans La/April 1861"

Rudolph Lux practiced the very distinguished European art form of painting and gilding porcelain, which enjoyed very little note in mid-nineteenth century America. Never the less, he is considered to be the most successful artist of his type working in the Old South. His highly detailed and well-wrought images of figures both civic and domestic were much prized in New Orleans, where he worked in both the French Quarter and the American section.

After the capitulation of New Orleans in 1862 Lux painted several members of the occupying forces, notably Nathaniel Banks, Benjamin F. Butler, and David Farragut. But prior to that time, internal evidence on this plate indicates that he created a series of works commemorating secession. This particular plate has an iconography composed of eight stars representing the eight Southern States who formed the Confederacy: South Carolina, Mississippi, Florida, Alabama, Georgia, Louisiana, Texas, and Virginia.

The member of a prominent Jewish family and an equally powerful political figure in his own right, Judah P. Benjamin was an appropriate subject for Lux. Having served Louisiana as a senator, he subsequently served as Secretary of War and Secretary of State for the Confederate States of America from March 1862 until the demise of the C.S.A. in April 1865.

Benjamin was widely considered to be the most intelligent and effective member of President Davis' cabinet. Confederate historian Clement Eaton has written that Benjamin was "extremely versatile, he had the virtue of detachment and made a judicious counselor." Unregenerate and certainly unreconstructed, Benjamin fled to England after the war where he practiced law until his death.

EDWARD EVERARD ARNOLD (circa 1816-1866)

Born, Heilbronn, Germany; studied lithography in Germany; active in New Orleans, circa 1850-1866; died, New Orleans.

Admiral Farragut's Entrance into Mobile Bay, the Morning of August 5, 1864

Oil on canvas
30 x 40 inches
Inscribed at bottom:
SELMA MORGAN GAINES RAM TENNESSEE FORT MORGAN TECUMSEH T.A.M. Craven Comder [Commander], BROOKLYN James Alden Capt. OCTORARA C.H. Green L. Comder MANHATTAN J.W.A. Nicholson Comder WINNEBAGO T.H. Stevens Comder HARTFORD Percival D. Rayton Capt. METACOMET J.E. Jouett Lt. Comder CHICKASAW T.H. Perkins Lt. Com. RICHMOND T.A. Jenkins Capt. PORT ROYAL B. Gherardi Lt. Comder LACKAWANNA J.B. Marchand Capt. SEMINOLA E. Donaldson Comder OSSIPEE W.E. LeRoy Comder ITASCA George Brown Lt. Comder ONEIDA J.R.N. Mullane Comder GALENA C.H. WELLS Lt. Comder Painted by E. Arnold
Circa 1864

PROVENANCE:
Estate of Sara M.B. Roby, Nantucket, Massachusetts until 1987

Arnold, a native of Heilbronn, Germany, first appeared in New Orleans in 1850. For the next ten years he worked in various capacities: sign-painter, lithographer, and part-time fancy painter. His most ambitious project, a panoramic view of New Orleans created in conjunction with his partner James Guy Evans, never materialized.

Arnold's abilities as an engraver are more than apparent in his major marine paintings. These are almost always characterized by a highly defined linear quality which sharply defined the planes and placement of objects within the view. When essaying an important historical topic like the Battle of Port Hudson on the Mississippi River, or the entrance of Farragut into Mobile Bay, this definition assists in the organization of the broad and varied material.

While a critical moment in Southern history, the Yankee admiral's triumphant processional into Mobile was hardly good news for the war-torn Confederacy. With the Mississippi effectively controlled by Union forces and the city of Mobile cut off, all hope of foreign aid for the South was abandoned, undoubtedly shortening the war considerably.

One might suppose that the event did afford both Arnold his best moment as a painter and Farragut his finest moment as a character. Lashed to the rigging of his flagship, he is said to have cried, "Damn the torpedoes, full speed ahead!" when his fellow ships hesitated before the Confederate torpedo line. History, which tends to be written–or at least printed by the victorious, has not revealed the notable quotes of Farragut's Confederate opponent.

JOHN ROSS KEY (1832-1920)

Born, Hagerstown, Maryland; studied in Munich, Paris, and at the National Academy of Design, 1856-1857; active in Charleston, South Carolina, 1863-1865; and in Baltimore throughout his career; died, Baltimore.

Fort Sumter

Oil on canvas
9 1/4 x 14 1/2 inches
Remnant of signature lower left
Circa 1865

PROVENANCE:
Private collection, Greenville, South Carolina until 1991

RELATED LITERATURE:
Alfred C. Harrison, Jr., "Bierstadt's *Bombardment of Fort Sumter* reattributed," *The Magazine Antiques*, February 1986, 415-422.

Like many of his fellow citizens of Maryland, John Ross Key, a descendant of Francis Scott Key, chose to fight for the Confederacy when war broke out between the North and the South. As much of his early experience as an artist involved mapmaking and charting for the United States Coastal Survey, his talents were put to use for ordnance purposes in the Charleston theatre of action during the final years of the war.

As a second lieutenant Key rendered several drawings of Charleston harbor and Fort Sumter. Many of these came to the attention of General Beauregard, Confederate commander at Charleston, who felt Key was "a young artist of great promise" and appointed him to a committee compiling a "military history of the siege of Charleston." These sketches became the basis for a number of major paintings by Key, including the well-known *Bombardment of Fort Sumter* once attributed to Albert Bierstadt and now in the collection of the Greenville County (South Carolina) Museum of Art.

In a landmark article re-attributing the work to Key, Alfred C. Harrison, Jr. weights certain critical responses to the artist's work. Key's style reflects a rather creative assimilation of prevailing notions of history painting with the realistic tendencies then nascent in larger Western art. Harrison notes that in his larger work on the bombardment, Key "did not choose to relieve the cold expanse of sea and sky with the warmth of conventional clouds, or to idealize the scene to the extent expected by the picturesque tradition."

So it is that in this smaller work Key enhances, rather than mitigates, the somewhat stark qualities of the large block-like fortress floating upon the vast, still salt waters of the inner harbor. While a stunningly realistic evocation of the actual site, it is also a haunting reminder of one of the most dramatic settings in all of Southern history.

51

ESTEBAN CHARTRAND (1825-1889)

Born, Cuba; active in Charleston, South Carolina, circa 1870; died ?

Sunset at the Savanna's, South Carolina

Oil on canvas
24 1/4 x 44 inches
Inscribed on the reverse prior to lining:
Sunset at the Savanna's, South Carolina; To Dr. M. Michel. M.D. Charleston, So. Ca. This Picture is Respectfully Dedicated. By the author may-anno MDCCCLXX. (1870).

A Cuban artist in the Barbizon mood, Esteban Chartrand's landscape art enjoyed considerable success in his native land. Art historian Gary Libby has pointed out that Chartrand's "type of sentimental landscape eulogized the palm tree and the small stream, and was destined to a long and popular life in Cuban art."

Like Joseph Rusling Meeker and the equally elusive George F. Higgins, Chartrand paints in a style which enhances the natural mystery of the tropical landscape, which, unlike its Hudson River School counterpart, never lends itself entirely to a tamed aesthetic of total beauty. That the rough, slightly threatening air of the terrain could be so wonderfully captured is a tribute to both the artist's ability and the dimensions of the setting itself.

PROVENANCE:
Middleton Michel, MD, Charleston, South Carolina, 1870; Robertson Family of Bull Street, Charleston; Edith Phin, Charleston; Phyllis Baker, Columbia, South Carolina until 1989

RELATED LITERATURE:
Gary Libby, "Cuban Masters," *International Fine Arts Collector,* January 1991, 48-55.

51

EVERETT B.D. JULIO (1843-1879)

Born, British colony of St. Helena Island; studied in Boston with William Rimmer, 1861-1864; active in New Orleans, 1869-1879; died, Kingston, Georgia.

The Last Meeting of Lee and Jackson

Oil on canvas
13 feet 10 3/4 inches x 9 feet 7 inches including frame
Signed and dated lower left: Julio St. Louis Mo. 1869

PROVENANCE:
The Wagener Gallery, New Orleans, Louisiana; Colonel John B. Richardson, New Orleans until 1910; Colonel James Butterfield Sinnott, New Orleans; Charles Sinnott, New Orleans until 1987

EXHIBITIONS:
Washington Artillery Hall, New Orleans, Louisiana until 1910.
 Louisiana State Museum, New Orleans, Louisiana until 1956.
 On extended tour to Museum of the Confederacy, Richmond, Virginia; Greenville County Museum of Art, Greenville, South Carolina; Alabama Department of Archives and History, Montgomery, Alabama; Tennessee State Museum, Nashville, Tennessee; Memphis Brooks, Memphis, Tennessee; Mississippi Museum of Art, Jackson, Mississippi; Fine Arts Museum of the South, Mobile, Alabama; Madison-Morgan Cultural Center, Madison, Georgia: 1988-1989.

LITERATURE:
Ken Burns, *The Civil War*, episode IV (Washington, D.C.: WETA-TV and Florentine Films, 1989).
 William H. Gerdts, *Art Across America, Two Centuries of Regional Painting 1710-1920*, vol. 2 (New York: Abbeville Press, Publishers, 1990), 102-103 (reproduced).
 Estill Curtis Pennington, *The Last Meeting's Lost Cause* (Spartanburg, South Carolina: Robert M. Hicklin Jr., Inc., 1988), 24 (reproduced).
 (A more comprehensive listing is available upon request.)

The circumstances of the last meeting of Confederate Generals Lee and Jackson are quite well-known and represent one of the most evocative aspects of the military history of the South. As they conferred in the early morning hours of May 2, 1863, neither of these old soldiers could have realized that they faced their most important, and indeed final, significant victory. Nor could they have known that Jackson would soon be dead.

Immortal as that meeting, the generals are well served by Julio's talents. Consider that Julio was only twenty-five years old when he began to compose one of the largest and most ambitious history paintings ever created in this country. In sheer scale alone the work is monumental, a gigantism which is in no way compromised by the artist's superbly realized mounted equestrian figures.

Julio was equally accurate in historical detail and painterly device. The mounts reflect ongoing trends in Western art depicting horse and rider. Nor has any serious critique ever been delivered against the facial likenesses of both main figures. Drawing upon contemporary photographs and engravings, Julio created a Lee and Jackson virtually indistinguishable from life sittings.

Amazingly enough, Julio was also sufficiently equipped as an entrepreneur to move this enormous work from St. Louis to Memphis to New Orleans, setting it up and taking it down several times for purposes of display to large crowds of Southerners anxious for an evocative glimpse of the heroes of the Lost Cause. While unsuccessful in selling the work in his own time, Julio created a graphic image which has come to embody the very spirit of the Confederacy in victory and defeat. He has set the actual figures in a landscape of mythic proportion, freezing them there before the immediacy of death, victory, or defeat. In many respects *The Last Meeting* is the single most important history painting based on an episode in the cultural life of the South.

ESTEBAN CHARTRAND (1825-1889)

Born, Cuba; active in Charleston, South Carolina, circa 1870; died ?

Sunset at the Savanna's, South Carolina

Oil on canvas
24 1/4 x 44 inches
Inscribed on the reverse prior to lining:
Sunset at the Savanna's, South Carolina; To Dr. M. Michel. M.D. Charleston, So. Ca. This Picture is Respectfully Dedicated. By the author may-anno MDCCCLXX. (1870).

A Cuban artist in the Barbizon mood, Esteban Chartrand's landscape art enjoyed considerable success in his native land. Art historian Gary Libby has pointed out that Chartrand's "type of sentimental landscape eulogized the palm tree and the small stream, and was destined to a long and popular life in Cuban art."

Like Joseph Rusling Meeker and the equally elusive George F. Higgins, Chartrand paints in a style which enhances the natural mystery of the tropical landscape, which, unlike its Hudson River School counterpart, never lends itself entirely to a tamed aesthetic of total beauty. That the rough, slightly threatening air of the terrain could be so wonderfully captured is a tribute to both the artist's ability and the dimensions of the setting itself.

PROVENANCE:
Middleton Michel, MD, Charleston, South Carolina, 1870; Robertson Family of Bull Street, Charleston; Edith Phin, Charleston; Phyllis Baker, Columbia, South Carolina until 1989

RELATED LITERATURE:
Gary Libby, "Cuban Masters," *International Fine Arts Collector*, January 1991, 48-55.

W.H. LANGWORTHY
(working circa 1873)

Born, ?; known to have been active in Virginia, circa 1873; died ?

Natural Bridge, Virginia

Oil on canvas
36 x 29 inches
Signed and dated lower center:
W H Langworthy. 1873

RELATED LITERATURE:
Pamela H. Simpson, *So Beautiful an Arch: Images of the Natural Bridge, 1787-1890* (Lexington, Virginia: Washington and Lee University, 1982).

The Natural Bridge of Virginia was thought to be the most astonishing place in nature in the ante-bellum South, a site so special as to evoke the eighteenth century sense of the sublime. No less than Thomas Jefferson, who once owned this bridge washed from rock by coursing waters, felt that, "It is impossible for the emotions, arising from the sublime to be felt beyond what they are here: so beautiful an arch, so elevated, so light, springing as it were up to heaven! The rapture of the spectator is really indescribable!"

Several major nineteenth century artists painted the bridge, including Frederick Edwin Church and David Johnson. Both of these artists painted scenes that emphasized the great natural wonder in realistic terms, setting it in a great expanse of landscape, and focusing upon the peculiar topography of the area.

Langworthy's representation of the natural bridge is far more unique, speaking to the Gothic imagination of the Romantic era rather than to the cool, tidy spirit of the eighteenth century sublime. Here, the bridge soars upwards with a forceful verticality strengthened by the simple frontality of the composition. Mood and coloration recall the feel of a Gothic cathedral, a favorite metaphor of the age. His coloration is dramatic, almost eerie, forcing the viewer to look within and beyond the merely two-dimensional, to revel in the grandeur of this special Southern place.

THOMAS SATTERWHITE NOBLE (1835-1907)

Born, Lexington, Kentucky; studied in Paris with Thomas Couture, 1853; active in St. Louis and New York; headmaster of McMicken School of Art, Cincinnati, Ohio, 1868-1904; died, New York City.

The Jester

Oil on canvas, 35 x 25 inches
Signed and dated lower left: T.S. Noble. 1877

PROVENANCE:

Jack Geis (the artist's grandson), Georgetown, Kentucky until 1989

EXHIBITIONS:

Cincinnati Art Museum, Cincinnati, Ohio, *Exhibition of the Work of the Late Thomas S. Noble . . .*, 1907, no. 26.

Art Institute of Chicago, Chicago, Illinois, *Paintings by Thomas S. Noble*, 1908, no. 26.

St. Louis Museum of Fine Arts, St. Louis, Missouri, *Paintings by Thomas S. Noble*, et. al., 1908, no. 26.

Ralston Galleries, New York, *Paintings by Thomas S. Noble*, 1910.

Owensboro Museum of Fine Arts, Owensboro, Kentucky, *Kentucky Expatriates: Natives and Notable Visitors*, 1984, no. 67.

University of Kentucky Art Museum, Lexington, Kentucky; Greenville County Museum of Art, Greenville, South Carolina; Art Academy of Cincinnati, Cincinnati, Ohio: *Thomas Satterwhite Noble, 1835-1905*, 1988.

Cheekwood Fine Arts Center, Nashville, Tennessee, *Wishful Thinking: Victorian Themes in Southern Painting*, 1991-1992.

LITERATURE:

James D. Birchfield, "Thomas S. Noble: 'Made for a Painter'" Part II, *The Kentucky Review* 6 (Summer 1986): 63 (reproduced).

James D. Birchfield, Albert Boime, and William J. Hennessey, *Thomas Satterwhite Noble, 1835-1907* (Lexington, Kentucky: University of Kentucky Art Museum, 1988), 88 (reproduced).

Kentucky Expatriates: Natives and Notable Visitors (Owensboro, Kentucky: Owensboro Museum of Fine Arts, 1984), 115 (reproduced).

Bettye Lee Mastin, "Kentucky Homes," *Lexington [Kentucky] Herald Leader*, 12 February 1983.

A native of Lexington, Kentucky, Noble trained in France with the didactic history painter Thomas Couture. Couture was a great master at elaborate compositions with compelling hidden meanings of allegorical import, a trait which Noble absorbed and occasionally displays. Couture's influence is certainly apparent in two of Noble's most famous works, *The Price of Blood* and *The Last Slave Auction*, both of which are manifestations of Noble's deep aversion to that labor system which brought down Southern civilization.

However, like other artists who worked in revivalist modes for a high Victorian audience which delighted in costume pageants, Noble often painted works with a less didactic historical sweep. *The Jester* comes from Noble's middle period when medieval, renaissance, and ancient themes supplanted his contemporary social images.

Noble may have been inspired, in part, by his master teacher Couture as regards subject and costume in this piece. In 1857 Couture painted a number of variations of two men posed in baroque counterpoint and dressed in the costumes of the harlequinade. Couture's jester figure sits with his back to the viewer, however, facing a white robed Pierot figure.

According to the exhibition catalog *Thomas S. Noble*, "the composition of this work and family tradition hold that the picture once had a pendant to clarify the artist's intended meaning." While it is true that a pendant would resolve the absent gaze of the splendidly garbed jester, it really isn't altogether necessary. The absence of a pendant creates a powerful sense of wonder as the jester, with a wry and knowing look, stares absently toward a court we cannot see presided over by a ruler we will never know.

ANDREW JOHN HENRY WAY (1826-1888)

Born, Washington, D.C.; studied with John P. Frankenstein in Cincinnati and with Alfred Jacob Miller in Baltimore before studies in France and Italy, 1850-1854; active in Baltimore throughout his career; died, Baltimore.

Apples and Pottery

Oil on canvas
16 x 14 inches
Signed lower left:
AJH Way
Circa 1880

Little in Way's early education and initial personal success prepare the viewer for the subtle, connoisseur qualities of this charming still life. Way was brought along in the florabunda tradition of American still life art by masters like John Frankenstein and Alfred Jacob Miller, artists with strong narrative and trompe l'oeil tendencies. Way himself gained greatest note for his "portraits" of grapes, ripe and hanging on the vine, glistening with moisture and emoting a high Victorian reality reeking of pathetic fallacy.

Here we find that Way has returned to the true roots of that Maryland still life art of which he was the most outstanding practitioner in the late nineteenth century. Like the Peales, in particular James and Raphaelle, Way has found neo-classical perfection in a restrained, minimal composition.

On this very intimate level the apples offer a bold statement by their very loose placement on the table in close proximity to the pieces of ceramics. The ceramics themselves are evidence that the work is from Way's late period when he occasionally deviated from his more typical subject of grapes. The subtle, slight line of red down the left side of the ceramic vase is a strong pictorial element, setting the piece in high relief.

WILLIAM AIKEN WALKER (1839-1921)

Born, Charleston, South Carolina; active in Charleston; Baltimore, Maryland; Louisville, Kentucky; Augusta, Georgia; New Orleans, Louisiana; Galveston, Texas; and in various Southern resorts, including Arden, North Carolina and Ponce Park, Florida throughout his life; died, Charleston.

Sarah and Jeremiah

Oil on canvas
each 18 x 10 inches
Each signed lower left: WAWalker
Circa 1885

PROVENANCE:
Newman Galleries, Philadelphia, Pennsylvania; Robert M. Hicklin Jr., Inc., Spartanburg, South Carolina; D. Van Smith, Charleston, South Carolina until 1991

EXHIBITIONS:
Gibbes Museum of Art, Charleston, South Carolina, William Aiken Walker: From Southern Collections, 1986.

LITERATURE:
These works will be included in Cynthia Seibels' forthcoming book on the artist.

A native of the South's crown city of Charleston, William Aiken Walker discovered his signature Southern themes in the revived, post-Reconstruction economy of the 1880s and 90s. Cotton fields, cotton bales stacked high on the levee of the Mississippi River, wagons of cotton drawn by mules down back-country dirt roads, black cotton pickers, and the dilapidated shacks they inhabited dominated Walker's work in this period. He won the highest praise and greatest monetary rewards for these subjects, labelled by one commentator as "intensely southern scenes."

Sarah and *Jeremiah* are typical of Walker's renderings of black sharecroppers, a theme he began to pursue with vigor in 1885. True to his formula for such subjects, each figure is placed in the extreme forefront of the picture plane standing upon a patch of dirt at the edge of a cotton field in full bloom. Their tattered, ill-fitting garments suggest extreme poverty, yet their facial expressions suggest contentment with their lot in life—a perception that Walker and other whites chose to see. *Sarah* and *Jeremiah* were painted not to immortalize two individuals but rather to depict characters who were viewed at the time as quintessential aspects of the Cotton Kingdom.

JOSEPH RUSLING MEEKER (1827-1889)

Born, Newark, New Jersey; studied at the National Academy of Design, 1845; active in Louisville, Kentucky, 1852-1859; and in Louisiana, 1862-1865; thought to have made intermittent sketching trips to the Mississippi Delta area, 1865-1875; died, St. Louis, Missouri.

Solitary Pirogue by the Bayou

Oil on canvas
17 3/4 x 30 inches
Signed and dated lower right: JR Meeker 86

As a paymaster on a Union gunboat during the War Between the States, Meeker spent countless hours patrolling Louisiana swampland. Throughout his career, Meeker drew on this experience as a source of inspiration for his art. The author of several marvelous articles on his personal artistic vision, Meeker leaves little doubt as to his passionate search for "an area of repose."

It is tempting to describe Meeker's artistic development as reminiscent of the change in light that marks day's passage from dawn to dusk. His earliest swamp pictures have the rather vivid intensity of discovery—of the new day— while his later pictures have a twilight effect. These are often moody in the tonalist manner so prevalent after the rise of the Salmagundi Club school. During this same later period Meeker often resorted to formulaic compositions based upon previous successes, giving the body of his work a somewhat sadly frayed, commercial quality.

However, none of those elements are present in this unique composition. While a very late picture, it has, nevertheless, the brilliant, dramatic light of Meeker's best early work. A quiescence of light softly divides the mass of trees on the left from the shimmering grove in the distant swamp. Motifs from Meeker's *Evangeline* picture make a return in the form of the man standing in the pirogue near the middle ground of the picture plane.

Perhaps most importantly, the entire representation of trees on the left has the look and feel of the Louisiana school, particularly the humidity-drenched weeping live oak, elusively mirrored in the water below. Like Richard Clague, Charles Giroux, and Andreas Molinary, Meeker has been to the swamp and seen the light, returning there as often as the painters of the Hudson River returned to the Catskills for renewal.

HERMAN HERZOG
(1832-1932)

Born, Bremen, Germany; trained in the Dusseldorf Academy with Achenbach; active in Florida, 1885-1910; died, Philadelphia.

Heron's Rest

Oil on canvas
26 x 22 inches
Signed lower left:
H. Herzog
Circa 1890

The clear light apparent in this work testifies to Herman Herzog's training in the Dusseldorf, Germany school of painting. Having reached a certain notoriety in Europe before coming to America, Herzog can be seen as one of those artists who reverses the normal process of expatriation in our culture, becoming a missionary rather than a refugee.

Herzog's visits to Florida between 1885 and 1910, trips made by train to see his son John in Gainesville, resulted in some of his most profound achievements as a painter. Like Martin Johnson Heade he brought a slightly retarded style to the swamps and flatlands of north Florida, imbued with the lingering light of international romantic luminism and altogether appropriate for the exotic locales he so loved to record.

Several of his contemporaries, notably George Herbert McCord, developed certain formulaic approaches to landscape art in Florida, particularly the use of certain ongoing naturalistic devices which assume a semiotic importance. In Herzog's art this is most detectable in certain recurring bird motifs. Herzog frequently used herons, both in flight and at rest, to portray those moments of freedom and spontaneity in nature which so enliven the artist's work.

RUFUS WAY SMITH
(working circa 1890)

Treme Market, New Orleans

Oil on canvas
16 x 12 inches
Signed and dated lower left:
R. Way Smith '90.

Internal evidence suggests that the scene at hand depicts the French Market in New Orleans located in the lower quarter below the St. Louis Cathedral, perhaps in the vicinity of Governor Nichols and Decatur Streets. The paving blocks and balconies resemble those on Decatur Street as does the open shed, although it is not the famous portico designed by Gallier for the same area. The presence of fruit and shoppers is a vivid reminder of the function the market served as a venue for the goods of South America as well as the Deep South.

CHARLES SIDNEY RALEIGH (1830-1925)

Born, Gloucester, England; lengthy career as merchant seaman, including service in the United States Navy; entirely self-taught; active in New Bedford, Massachusetts; died, New Bedford.

Engagement Between the Cumberland and the Merrimac

Oil on canvas
51 1/2 x 86 3/4 inches
Signed and dated lower left:
C.S. Raleigh. 1893

PROVENANCE:
Cumberland Association, Kendrick House, Wareham, Massachusetts about 1893; Naval Reserve Unit, New Bedford, Massachusetts; Whaling Museum, New Bedford, Massachusetts, 1962 until 1985

Charles Raleigh certainly came by his interest in marine painting honestly. A merchant seaman for thirty years before settling down to a career as an artist, once Raleigh began to paint, his output was prodigious. Considering that he was primarily self-taught, the large scale of his work, the strong coloration, and the proper balance between proportions is most impressive.

This huge image of the engagement between the *Cumberland* and the *Merrimac* is one of Raleigh's finest efforts. The battle itself marked one of the more significant victories for the sparse and fledgling Confederate Navy. During the winter of 1862 the Union successfully created a blockade of Hampton Roads, Virginia, effectively cutting Norfolk off as the South's principal eastern port. To remedy that situation, Captain Franklin Buchanan steamed into the area on March 8, 1862. Ramming both the *U.S.S. Cumberland* and the *Congress*, which were being used as wooden blockade vessels, Buchanan was successful in sinking both and freeing the port, at least temporarily. He was subsequently promoted to the rank of Admiral.

Raleigh's work has a very strong frontality that parallels the movement of the ironclad with the tilt of the wooden vessel about to go under. Equally strong is the presence of the vessel on the left whose lead lines create a dramatic ninety-degree angle enhancing depth and perspective.

WILLIAM GILBERT GAUL (1855-1919)

Born, Jersey City, New Jersey; studied with John George Brown and at the National Academy of Design, New York; active in Van Buren County, Tennessee, 1881-1904; and in Nashville, 1905-1907; died, Ridgefield Park, New Jersey.

A Hunter's Toast and Young Girl in Interior
(see page 75)

Oil on canvas
24 x 18 inches each
Hunter's Toast signed and dated:
Copyright 1903 by Gilbert Gaul
Young Girl signed:
Gilbert Gaul
1903

During his lifetime, Gaul was praised by the critic George Parsons Lathrop in *The Quarterly Illustrator* as "one of the best known of our American illustrators" for his works depicting various episodes in American military history. At the same time Lathrop points out that Gaul "gained renown in the treatment of two almost distinct classes of figure subjects. . . ."

While much of Gaul's subsequent reputation is based on history paintings with a military flavor, especially his Southern series *With the Confederate Colors*, he was actually an artist of very diversified ability. Inspired by the local setting of his rural Tennessee farm near Van Buren, he created several impressive landscapes in the impressionist style. At the same time his observations on the local inhabitants of Van Buren proved sufficiently amusing to prompt a number of genre paintings of the type at hand.

A Hunter's Toast and *Young Girl in Interior* were created with a very specific audience in mind. At the beginning of this century the picturesque literature of the rural South was a powerful market force in publishing circles. Southern writers like John Fox, Jr. and James Lane Allen produced works that celebrated backwoods virtues acted out against a backdrop of simple, sentimental attachment to place and family.

Gaul's two paintings are very much a part of that affection. The comfortable old hunters in the log cabin setting are quaint reminders of the

(continued on page 74)

WILLIAM GILBERT GAUL (*continued from page 72*)

EXHIBITIONS:
Robert M. Hicklin Jr., Inc., Spartanburg, South Carolina; Thomasville Cultural Center, Thomasville, Georgia; Swan Coach House Gallery, Atlanta, Georgia: *At Break of Dawn: Sporting Art in the South*, 1989-1990.

Presbyterian College, Clinton, South Carolina, *Southern Visions*, 1991.

rural past quickly vanishing from industrial America. The discreetly appealing young girl in her old-fashioned bonnet is another manifestation of nostalgic genre painting in the manner of John George Brown and Edward Lamson Henry.

Curiously enough, the rural South became a nostalgic repository for the sentimental longings of the national imagination. These Southern hunters and the pensive child represent an unspoiled quality in the American character—an ironic conclusion in the aftermath of the War Between the States and economic deprivation.

JOHN GUTZON BORGLUM (1867-1941)

Born, Bear Lake, Idaho; studied at the San Francisco Art Association; active in California, New York, and in Atlanta, 1916-1924; died, Chicago.

Stonewall Jackson

Portrait bust in plaster
26 inches high x 13 1/2 inches wide x 13 inches deep
Inscribed: Gutzon Borglum 1923

PROVENANCE:
Private collection, San Diego, California until 1988

RELATED EXAMPLE:
The Stamford Museum, Stamford, Connecticut, *Exhibition of Sculpture by Gutzon Borglum*, 1963, no. 6.

Borglum spent his youth and young adulthood studying in San Francisco and at the Academie Julien in Paris, France. While there he became enamored of the French avant-garde realist Auguste Rodin, whose monumentalism greatly impressed Borglum. Near the end of the century Borglum returned to this country and began to create works that were far more monumental in scale, and far less emotive in empathic feeling for the subject matter. He quickly became the sculptor of choice for a number of important public works, notably the Sheridan monument in Washington D.C.

During the late nineteenth and early twentieth centuries in this country most of the intellectual and artistic community embraced the concept of the "white city," a civic planning impulse that stressed the importance of parks, wide avenues, and large commemorative sculpture. It was this era of gigantism in stone that led the Atlanta Chapter of the United Daughters of the Confederacy to commission Borglum to carve a depiction of General Lee onto the exposed granite walls of Stone Mountain Georgia, an unrivaled natural phenomenon of tremendous scale. This experience would later inspire Borglum to create the heroic presidential monument at Mount Rushmore, a project he initiated, designed, and directed.

From the outset the ladies of the U.D.C. should have feared the worst, for Borglum quickly created a design that included Lee, Stonewall Jackson, and Jefferson Davis in an elaborate pose that reeked of high Victorian heroism. While the artist faithfully pursued his vision, the First World War and lack of funding quickly curtailed the project. While the head of Lee was unveiled on January 19, 1924, the rest of the project was placed on hold as the result of Borglum's dramatic flight from Atlanta, one step ahead of a posse, later that same year. Half a century later it was still only partially complete.

Borglum's source for the likeness of Jackson was almost certainly the celebrated lithograph by Ernest Crehen, published in Richmond, Virginia in 1863. Crehen used a photograph of Jackson taken some two weeks before his death, showing the General in strong profile. Borglum's model of Jackson's head, in three dimensions, has a strong, French, Second Empire feel. Jackson's Old Testament beard has taken on a French imperial shape, although he looks appropriately grave and severe, especially when one ponders his knotted brow and vague, distant look.

ELIOT CANDEE CLARK (1883-1980)

Born, New York City; studied with his father, the tonalist painter Walter Clark; active in Savannah, Georgia, 1923-1924; and in Albemarle County, Virginia from 1932 until his death; died, Charlottesville, Virginia.

Spanish Moss, Savannah

Oil on canvas
31 3/4 x 40 inches
Signed lower right:
Eliot Clark
1923-24

PROVENANCE:

Mrs. Eliot Clark, Charlottesville, Virginia; Don Lewis, Norfolk, Virginia; Margaret Mayo, Gloucester, Virginia until 1991

Eliot Clark spent the winters of 1923 and 1924 in Savannah, Georgia, where he had been invited to teach at the Savannah Art Club. In a biographical account of the artist's life written by his second wife, Margaret Fowler Clark, it is noted that the setting provided the artist with great inspiration. "During those Savannah winters he painted many of his finest works, the waterfront at twilight, old homes and landmarks, marvelous great trees, colorful warehouses in the half-light, and so on."

As Clark was trained in the tonalist mood by his father, the painter Walter Clark, it is not surprising to find a certain harmonic color value in this work of "marvelous great trees." Clark also admired Whistler's work, to the extent of including in his chapbook one of that artist's remarks on the value of mist and twilight as an atmospheric setting, the time when "evening mist clothes the riverside with poetry."

Clark exhibited several of his Savannah works at the Telfair Academy in 1924 to considerable local acclaim. One local critic, Jane Judge, praised them for "an interpretation of nature . . . in the mood of lyricism, romance, wistfulness." Like other Southern landscape artists before him, Clark found in the looming live oak a presence that transcended mere nature to become an inhabitant on the scene.

ALFRED HEBER HUTTY (1877-1954)

Born, Grand Haven, Michigan; studied at the St. Louis School of Fine Arts, 1892; and with Lowell Birge Harrison at the New York Art Students League in Woodstock, New York, 1907; worked as a stained glass designer for Tiffany's; active in Charleston, South Carolina, 1920-1954; died, Woodstock.

The Red Bud

Oil on canvas
32 x 40 inches
Signed lower right:
Alfred Hutty
Circa 1925

PROVENANCE:

Private collection, Fort Walton Beach, Florida until 1991

Alfred Hutty's famous wire to his wife to "come quickly, have found heaven" epitomizes his sympathetic feelings for the city of Charleston, South Carolina. Hutty's move to Charleston during the 1920s coincided with that renaissance in the arts which has come to be recognized as a crowning achievement in the city's cultural history.

Primarily known as an etcher and draftsman, Hutty was able to create the infrequent, but quite brilliant, oil. His emotive response to Charleston sprang from an obvious affection for the texture and muted color of the ancient city's architecture and people. When he did paint, he applied the same bright, highly-keyed impressionist palette which so many artists of his age and training continued to use in the South right up until the Second World War.

This particular work is one of the artist's finest achievements, a sunny scene of the marsh country where Hutty frequently went on sketching tours. His drawings are reveries on the theme of live oaks hung with Spanish moss. This painting, however, is more about light and water interacting with the colors of the naturalistic habitat.

Several American critics and collectors responded to Hutty's atmospherics with praise. Stating the case most clearly was Duncan Phillips, who felt that, "There is no confusion between his aims" as a painter and as an etcher. "His paintings are painted and his etchings drawn."

KNUTE HELDNER (1875-1952)

Born, Vederlow Smoland, Sweden; studied at the Art Institute of Chicago; active in New Orleans, 1923-1952; died, New Orleans.

The Pig Woman– A Southern Idol

Oil on canvas
42 x 40 1/2 inches
Signed and dated lower right: Knute Heldner 32

PROVENANCE:
Duluth Art Institute, Duluth, Minnesota until 1990

After leading a rather colorful life in his native Sweden and in the American Midwest, Knute Heldner settled permanently in New Orleans in 1923. Once there he became something of a fixture in bohemian French Quarter life, creating numerous swamp paintings in his signature cool palette.

While these works capture something of the mystery of the bayou country, they are, by and large, formulaic representations which vary only in size and quantities of pirogues, shacks, and towering, moss-hung live oaks and cypress. His efforts at social realism, however, are in an altogether different style.

In the mid-1920s Heldner began to create works with an agenda of social concern characteristic of the American Scene Movement. Intended for a more select market than the tourist trade which bought his landscapes in the *Vieux Carre*, these "toil and the soil" pictures have a far more sensitive tone, one which recreates the hardships while revealing the innate nobility of the farm worker and the field hand.

The Pig Woman–A Southern Idol is in the same vein as another well-known work focusing upon a Southern black woman, Heldner's series of black madonnas. Departing from the tradition of Southern painters like William Aiken Walker and George Henry Clements, Heldner has chosen to present this black woman as a fully realized human being, not a hopeless caricature presented in styled costume.

WILL HENRY STEVENS (1881-1949)

Born, Vevay, Indiana; studied at the Cincinnati Art Academy, 1901-1904; active in New Orleans, and in Asheville, North Carolina, 1920-1949; died, New Orleans.

84 *Sevierville, Tennessee*

Oil on canvas
30 x 36 inches
Signed lower left:
Stevens
1946

PROVENANCE:
Private collection, Hendersonville, North Carolina until 1990

Stevens' progression from representation to abstraction is a well-known aspect of his development as a painter. Befitting his position as a member of the faculty at one of the finest art schools in the South, Tulane University in the days of the Woodward brothers, Stevens created a painterly style at once philosophic and avant-garde.

Like many academic abstractionists Stevens is firmly grounded in the color field shadings of Cezanne and the late impressionists. To his strongly edged line Stevens layers a certain stylistic pose adapted from his observations of Chinese art. Breaking down lines into strong intersections of color is also a characteristic of precisionism. Many of Stevens' works in the 1930s have a precisionist feel.

The work at hand shows Stevens on the cutting edge. Behind are the calm, peaceful scenes painted along the levee in New Orleans. Ahead are the warmly colored abstractions, reminiscent of Archille Gorky and Adolph Gottlieb. Viewing a valley town nestled on the edge of the Smokies, Stevens affirms the two-dimensional qualities of the picture plane by rendering the architectural structures as spiky, hard-edged forms, even as he creates depth and perspective by a strongly, slightly abstract frontality in scene and setting.

ANTHONY THIEME (1888-1954)

Born, Rotterdam, Holland; studied at the Academy of Fine Arts, Rotterdam, and at the Royal Academy, The Hague; active in Charleston, South Carolina, 1946-1947; and St. Augustine, Florida, 1947-1954; died, Pennsylvania.

St. Michael's, Charleston, SC

Oil on canvas
25 1/4 x 30 inches
Signed lower right:
A. Thieme
1946-47

Although Thieme's period of activity in Charleston was brief and quite late in his career, he did leave behind a personal perception of place in a series of paintings based on the architectural elements of the town. Applying a lingering impressionist eye to his subject matter was a well-chosen approach for the shimmering, humidity-filled port.

St. Michael's Church was a favorite topic for the artists of the Charleston Renaissance as well.

Index of Artists

	PAGE
John Abbot	30
Edward Everard Arnold	48
Edward Beyer	38
John Gutzon Borglum	76
Esteban Chartrand	54
Eliot Candee Clark	78
William Gilbert Gaul	72
Knute Heldner	82
Herman Herzog	66
Alfred Heber Hutty	80
Everett B.D. Julio	52
John Ross Key	50
W.H. Langworthy	56
Rudolph T. Lux	46
Joseph Rusling Meeker	64
Thomas Satterwhite Noble	58
Harriett Cany Peale	34
Charles Peale Polk	28
John J. Porter	42
Charles Sidney Raleigh	70
Thomas Addison Richards	32
Joachin Ferdinand Richardt	44
Rufus Way Smith	68
Will Henry Stevens	84
Anthony Thieme	86
Unknown	26
William Aiken Walker	62
Andrew John Henry Way	60
Thomas Wightman	36
Thomas Waterman Wood	40

5149

ROBERT M. HICKLIN JR., INC.
Fine Art of the American South

April 16, 1992

I am most pleased to send to you *Antiquarian Pursuits*, a commemorative catalog published in celebration of our twentieth anniversary. It features an introductory essay by Estill Curtis Pennington, as well as thirty-two works from our collection--each offered for sale, each with distinctive Southern associations.

Each piece of art presented is described in informative companion notes. It is often impossible, however, to include all the history available about the work in such a brief entry. Your inquiries are invited. Our staff is ready to provide details regarding condition, framing and quotations of price.

I hope this volume will be a meaningful addition to your reference library. It joins several other books published by the gallery, a list of which is printed on the verso of this sheet. Like its predecessors, *Antiquarian Pursuits* is designed to enlarge and enhance the study and appreciation of art of the American South. I trust you will find it enlightening.

Sincerely,

R.M. Hicklin, Jr
President

OTHER PUBLICATIONS BY ROBERT M. HICKLIN JR., INC.

Within the study of American art, it is assumed that any work produced upon this continent by an artist from any background is subject to consideration. Within the realm of Southern art as a more specific, subjective study, this is not so. Thus, locating a body of Southern art is a complex matter, made more complex by the fact that a mere cataloging of objects does not constitute a study of Southern art. Once found, these objects must be interpreted within the body of prevailing thought; it is necessary to seek Southern themes in Southern art objects, which must be subjected to the same scrutiny that has been applied to other aspects of Southern studies.

Estill Curtis Pennington,
Look Away: Reality and Sentiment in Southern Art

LOOK AWAY: REALITY AND SENTIMENT IN SOUTHERN ART is available for $54. post-paid. South Carolina residents add $2.50 state sales tax. 200 pages, 90 full color plates, hardbound.

ANTIQUARIAN PURSUITS By Estill Curtis Pennington. Featuring Southern art from the gallery's holdings in celebration of Robert M. Hicklin Jr., Inc.'s twentieth anniversary. 96 pages, 32 full color plates, softbound.

THE LAST MEETING'S LOST CAUSE By Estill Curtis Pennington. A definitive study of E.B.D. Julio's *The Last Meeting of Lee and Jackson* and its place in the icongraphy of the Southern experience. 67 pages, 25 plates, softbound.

THE SOUTH ON PAPER: LINE, COLOR AND LIGHT By James C. Kelly, Ph.D. An essential reference for anyone interested in Southern art. 155 pages, including biographical sketches on each of the 44 artists presented, 77 color plates, softbound.

HATTIE SAUSSY: GEORGIA PAINTER By Thetis B. Rush. This monograph includes a complete biography and 31 color plates. 38 pages, softbound.

Each of the above is available for $20 post-paid. South Carolina residents add $1.00 state sales tax.